First in the Series o~

Wedding Bells After Fifty

WE GOT MARRIED AND SO CAN YOU!

AUTUMN MARIE

ISBN 978-1-64299-955-6 (paperback)
ISBN 978-1-64299-956-3 (digital)

Christian Faith Publishing, Inc.
832 Park Avenue
Meadville, PA 16335
www.christianfaithpublishing.com

Printed in the United States of America

CONTENTS

INTRODUCTION

As It Turns Out, I Had Already Known My Future Husband for Seventeen Years

My own experience of remarrying inspired me to write this book. I was single in middle age and eventually found my ultimate soul mate. Working in the real estate industry, selling title and escrow services to realtors, investors, lenders, and builders, we do a lot of socializing. We get to know our clients, and I began to learn some of their stories—their lifestyles, their families, and the type of future they're trying to build for themselves or their companies. And then it's my job to connect them with the resources to make that happen. Along the way, traveling and getting to know so many people, I met many women over fifty who had successfully remarried. I realized that the idea that women can't remarry past a certain age is a myth. I hope that in some ways, sharing the stories of these women is like connecting my clients to the resources to build their lives and businesses. Only this time, I want to share what it takes to find a good second marriage. It can be done. It's happening all the time. We just need to stop perpetuating the idea that women over a certain age are less valuable.

It takes time to identify what you really want from a future relationship. This is a crucial part of building the self-confidence to maintain a good life while single. It's the same strength that will help you recognize when you've found a good future husband. They will make their intentions and character known with their actions, but you have to know your own worth first.

I learned this from personal experience. After the end of my first marriage, I was single for fifteen years before I married Michael. If I had known I would be single that long, well, it would have made the time in between marriages much more difficult. There were things I knew I needed from my next partnership. I'm very outgoing, very gregarious. I am interested in people, and I talk to strangers all the time. I needed someone who shared some of those qualities. I didn't want to feel alone in my work and social life anymore—I imagined being with someone who shared a similar lifestyle to mine that would enjoy accompanying me to events.

It's ironic that with work being so social, I didn't meet someone sooner, but my schedule of travel also made it difficult to really connect. At times, I enjoyed a life that was downright flashy, but still didn't like the idea of playing the field. I'm very particular. I was appreciating my independent financial success, though this went through ups and downs, and I knew what I wanted. I focused on making my life as fulfilling as possible without a husband, having a good time with my friends and putting my children first. Friends would tease me about being single for so long though. I was really picky—if I thought anybody was too young or not right, I would immediately just cut it off, not even give it a chance to start. I was keeping my eye out for a relationship that could lead to commitment, for a man who felt natural to be with. Sometimes I thought to myself, *Well, this is taking a very long time. Should it take this long? Am I ever going to meet anybody?*

As it turned out, I had already known my future husband for seventeen years. Michael was a client of mine, a commercial investor. I had never seen him as anything more than that, until things suddenly changed. Over a period of about three months, he had been inviting me to accompany him to sporting, social events, and parties. I had scheduling conflicts and couldn't attend. Eventually, I started to think, *What does this guy want?* As far as I knew, Michael was married; I'd met his wife in the past. Michael persisted. He asked me out to dinner on a night I had no conflicts, and I thought, *I don't know quite what is going on here, but he's a nice person and a client, so I should get together with him.* He insisted on picking me up to go to dinner. We lived nowhere near each other, and it was unusual enough to be going to dinner with a client. Lunches happened all the time, but not private dinners. I went along with it; in all the years we'd known each other, he'd always been professional, so I figured this guy is safe and upstanding. He said he went out of his way to pick a restaurant I hadn't been to before, since I had been to most restaurants in town. As dinner went on, he told me that he'd been trying to get together with me to tell me that he had split up with his wife some time ago. I just sat there thinking, *What a shame, such a nice guy, apparently interested in me*, and it followed my pattern that I was just not interested. But then when we were getting in the car to go home, our hands touched; and all of a sudden, I felt something I hadn't felt with him before. I paused, and everything I thought I knew about us fell away.

Everything just seemed to flow with us. We already shared a similar lifestyle and personality traits. He was very consistent. He knew what he wanted, and he wanted to be with me. It made things flow smoothly. He would touch bases with me on a regular basis, no games. He would call me most days and invite me to go out several times a week. As much as possible, we let things be easy. We had already been through other marriages and raised kids. There were a few small hiccups that tested our trust early in our relationship. We encountered the types of conflicts that are common at this stage of the game: dealing with the emotions of adult children and gauging your partner's fidelity while away traveling. It takes some awareness and confidence to remarry in your fifties. With us, things were very out in the open and consistent. In that way, we matched. After two-and-a-half years of dating, Michael proposed.

He'll forever tease me about how we were almost engaged in a hotel room in Reno. We were on a trip and had been so busy that by Sunday I just wanted to stay in and enjoy the beautiful suite we had booked. Michael was persistent. He convinced me to take a trip out to Lake Tahoe to his favorite restaurant on the lake. As soon as we arrived, Michael tried to order champagne, but I suggested we skip the champagne. He tried to convince me that I should start celebrating, and I still wasn't catching on. He said, "Do you know why I brought you here today?" I said, "Well, yes, because you really like this restaurant and you've been telling me it's the best." He replied, "No, I brought you here today to ask you to marry me." I started to cry. He knew me so well that he had bought me a cubic zirconia ring just so I would have something to wear in that moment, knowing I would want to pick out my own ring. And he also knew I would want to be able to say that we got engaged in such a gorgeous location.

As they say, the rest is history. I want to share the valuable insight that this kind of thing happens all the time. It's not a fairy tale. Real women find great, lasting partnerships at any age with men they can trust. Let's destroy the myth that if you're over fifty it can't happen. Your story might not look like mine—every story I've included in this book is different. Some people seem to have a knack for moving directly from one relationship to another, while others spend more time living on their own. Every woman's story showcases her own unique personality, and it is interesting to watch expectations change and grow. I hope this book serves to inspire women to move forward with everything they know is important for them, retain a sense of themselves, and have a clear idea of what they want and don't want from another marriage. No matter what stage of this process you're in, may this book keep you in good company!

Let's hear from my husband, Michael. When I asked him why he was interested in remarrying, it was surprising and endearing to find that men over fifty want to get married too! *I want to live my life to the fullest. I want someone to share my life with. Who wants to live and die by themselves? My friend died several years ago; and he had no wife, no children, and absolutely no one to give his prized possessions to. He had acquired so much and had so much success, but what was the point without love?"*

CHAPTER

1

Aurora: "Should I? Should I? Should I Not?"

When Aurora was in the process of ending a thirty-year marriage, she decided to try online dating. She said to herself that she was not the type of person to be alone. She had friends that had been through divorce; and in their bitterness or need for time apart, they would say, "Oh yeah, I was married back then, but now I know guys are all terrible and I'm happier alone." This just didn't ring true for her. She wanted to prove that she still had the confidence and power to attract good men and was curious about playing the field a bit. At the same time, she had been raised a "good Italian Catholic girl." The last time she had been single, she was quite young and had very traditional values. She still nurtured these in her fifties.

Curiosity got the better of her. Spending time online, she clicked on an ad for a dating site, repeating to herself, *Should I? Should I? Should I not?* She set up several meetings but was secretive about using online dating. She wasn't sure if she was "that type of woman," but more importantly, she needed time to privately feel out what it was like to be single and try to meet new men. If it was a travesty, she could at least keep it to herself. One of the first hurdles she encountered was selecting the age range she was willing to date within. Extremely young at heart and full of energy and enthusiasm, she decided that as long as the men were older than her grown children, a younger mate might be a good change of pace. Though online dating made her feel a bit more courageous and willing to flirt behind the shield of her computer screen, she never lied about her age. Her picture was current and accurate. Online dating was easier to get the hang of than she expected. She knew the minute her first marriage ended that it was over forever, so she gave herself license to experiment.

Her ex-husband had tried to stall the process of separating, asking, "What's the hurry?" Aurora just looked at him and said, "Do you know how old I am? I'm over fifty years old, and you're asking me what the hurry is? How dare you do this to me at my age." Aurora had three rules in her marriage that she had made very clear to her ex: no abuse, no drug use, and no cheating. He had broken the last rule and her trust. The marriage was otherwise very fulfilling, but the infidelity was insurmountable. And his unrepentant attitude once the affair was discovered made things worse. The blessing in this is that it made the decision to move on clear-cut for Aurora. It was a painful time, but she was sure of her decision.

She was also strengthened by her resolve to be a good mother. To her, this meant setting an example of courage and poise for her daughter and her sons. The children lost respect for their father, and the two parents stopped attending family events together. Aurora said to herself, "There are times in my life when I think I am not a strong person, but in this I have to be." She wanted to show her daughter, who was twenty years old at the time, that this would not destroy her. She was setting an example of feminine, motherly fortitude and resilience, even if on the inside she was struggling with the grief of divorce. It turned out to be a very powerful tactic; she acted her way into owning that strength.

She was living with her daughter, Ellen, in a rented apartment when she started talking to Jared online. It was a very new feeling for Aurora to live independently and learn to be by herself. So far, she had gone from being twenty-two years old and living at her parents' house to living with her first husband for thirty years. At fifty-two years old, she appreciated time to spend with her family and grow and see what she wanted. She liked the idea of meeting someone to go to dinner with occasionally and was excited by the coincidence that Jared lived in the same part of town. This seemed to take some of the guesswork out of a first meeting. In her first marriage, she had longed to spend more time traveling and on adventures, but her husband owned his own business, making time away very difficult. Jared asked her if she was adventurous about food, trying to pick a restaurant. She had never even tried Thai food. Their first meeting at a Thai restaurant set the stage for discovering that she could let go of her expectations for what she liked in a relationship. Sure, she was still a traditional girl in many ways, but maybe these days she was more flexible.

When they met for the first time at the Thai restaurant, things immediately felt different than they did with her other dates. This was already more of an adventure and was testing her sense of what she really valued. Jared had told her while chatting online that he was in the military. Although he had rented a house in La Mesa, he hadn't arrived yet. This had given her pause. She remembered that from way back when she was a little girl, she had told herself that she would never get involved with a fisherman or someone in the military. It wasn't so much that she worried about "too many ports of call" and the fidelity of long-distance relationships, but that she simply pictured herself as happier with someone who she could spend more one-on-one time with. She told Jared, "If I want someone in my life to keep me company, this defeats the purpose. I have a policy not to date anyone in the military." He replied, "Date? You haven't even met me yet." He took the upper hand in that argument and was persistent. They decided to meet around Valentine's Day. When she pulled into the parking lot, she immediately recognized him. Sitting across from him in the restaurant, she noticed that with the other men she had been out with, it felt more like fun and games. It had been easy to tell right away if she was interested or not interested in a way that felt almost too disposable. With Jared, she was nervous. She didn't know what to do with her hands. They would talk and then fall into silence. She thought to herself, *This is crashing all over the place*. On the way to their cars, he asked her on a second date.

Aurora developed the following certain rules for herself as she tried out online dating:

- *She knew she wanted to date someone that would have a more adventurous lifestyle.*
- *She wasn't willing to date anyone younger than her kids.*
- *She wanted to date someone local to avoid the pitfalls of long-distance courtship.*

Looking at her rules, what are some of your own criteria? What age group do you feel is right for you? What kind of activities do you enjoy sharing with a partner? What is the farthest you are willing to travel to meet up with someone? How often would you like to be able to see them? Remember you can make the decisions that are right for you, and if your criteria changes a bit as you meet new people, that's okay too. The partner you are looking for does not have to resemble your ex or someone you might have dated when you were younger. If your needs have changed, embrace them. You will experience better results with online dating if you "do it for you" first and foremost.

Aurora calls Jared "an American boy." He's in aviation electronics with the Navy, so he spends time assigned to ships maintaining the aircraft carried onboard. Throughout their early courtship, he was steady and assertive, always the one to set the next date. He was honest about his past and was interested in being a part of Aurora's family. As they got to know each other, she learned that Jared had made some poor lifestyle choices when he was much younger, getting involved in drugs and having a child at nineteen but not being present as a father. At the time they met, Jared was forty. Though younger than Aurora, it was clear from his demeanor and consistent communication that he had completely changed his lifestyle. He had even found his way back into supporting his daughter. Aurora told him about her three unbreakable rules for relationships: no drugs, no abuse, and no cheating. He said to her, "Aurora, I totally get it. If you're strong enough to walk away from someone you were with for thirty years, I think I believe your rules." His trustworthy attitude set the tone for their relationship and allowed Aurora to confront the distrust she had internalized from her divorce. She told Jared, "At the back of my mind, I'm always thinking, *How can I trust a person I just met when someone I trusted for thirty years, whom I thought would never hurt me, could cheat on me?*" Jared's response to this very difficult issue was, "I know this is hard, but I am going to be here and all I can do is try. You're just going to have to let go and let me prove to you that I'm not going to hurt you, that I do love you."

Part of how he demonstrated that love was by finding a way to offer Aurora security and proof of commitment despite his unusual schedule. His job required him to be away, stationed on a ship for weeks or months at a time. He also knew that in four years, he would be transferred. On the one hand, this ability to retain some independence during the early part of the relationship appealed to Aurora. She surprised herself by realizing that she would appreciate more time to learn to be by herself. On the other hand, how could she be sure that this relationship was going anywhere? She confessed to Jared that by the sound of it, their relationship had already been assigned a four-year lifespan. Finding out that he was about to start being deployed for five months at a time only added to the uncertainty. How would they keep it together? His response was to buy them a house. Aurora said, "Well, how is that going to work? I have a daughter." He answered, "No problem, it's a package deal."

Now, eight months into knowing each other and some of those spent apart, they started to look for a house. He bought it on his own but with her input and approval. Once he thought something was a good fit, he wanted her daughter and her parents to come see it and weigh in. He started to refer to Aurora's kids as his own and spend holidays with the group. Shortly after closing escrow, his parents came out, and Aurora met them. Starting to convert their relationship into a domestic partnership went very smoothly. Along the way, Aurora was still adapting to how she saw herself—both at this stage in her life and with a new partner. She continued to notice internal conflicts over her traditional upbringing, especially where her parents were involved. She moved along adapting to the situation. While he was away on deployment, she picked furniture for the house, arranging and combining what she and Jared already respectively owned. She hesitated to tell her parents she was moving in with Jared, expecting them to treat her like a little girl or perhaps still seeing herself that way. They were very accepting and saw that her past relationship had been strained for some time. They wanted her to have a chance at something more fulfilling. Aurora's instinct about their traditional viewpoint wasn't completely off, though. When her mother came to visit, she noticed that Aurora had put her larger bedroom set, a king size, in the master bedroom and put Jared's smaller set in the extra bedroom. Her mom said, "Oh, he doesn't mind that you put him in the guest room?" She looked at her mom and said, "You know we sleep together, right?" And just laughed it off.

Earlier in the relationship, a similar conflict had occurred. They had been dating for about a month when Jared invited Aurora to go to San Francisco and then to Napa Valley—a weekend away. Aurora assumed the invitation was just an offhand remark—something said hypothetically: Wouldn't it be nice if we got away? Jared had meant what he said. The very next morning, he sent her confirmation numbers for airline tickets, and she was shocked. She didn't know if she was ready to take the relationship to this level. The last man she had spent any serious intimate time with was her ex-husband. She also worried what her kids and parents would think about her going on vacation with a man she just met. Jared offered to cancel it but said that it seemed like she really wanted to go. She called her mom for approval, thinking how strange it was that she was fifty-two years old and feeling like a young girl. She was completely surprised by her mom's response, "That's nice. Go have fun."

With the partnership flowing smoothly and the house coming together, the remaining adjustments that needed to occur for this relationship to move forward were inside Aurora. She got more comfortable with the new home, and the times when Jared returned from deployment felt like playing house. Time apart also had a way of keeping the relationship fresh. They became more involved in each other's families and prepared to spend Christmas together. Jared took Aurora's daughter out shopping for a last-minute gift for her mother. Gestures like this made it easy to trust him more and more. She thought, *This is together. Even though we're not married, this is together.* They were living as if they were married. They had been dating for two years; but in reality, with Jared away so much, it had only been a few months.

The family gathered at their house for Christmas. They were about to start opening presents when Aurora's daughter, Ellen, insisted that they wait until her brother got there and started calling him on the phone, getting excited. When he arrived, they started opening gifts and having a relaxed breakfast. At the end of opening presents, Ellen insisted that Aurora open one last gift—a box of chocolates. Aurora assumed that they were from Ellen and that she just wanted to share them with everyone, so she fumbled with the wrappings. The box was completely sealed, and the ribbon was on tight, so as she yanked the box open, the cover popped off and something flew to the ground. Reaching down to pick it up, she realized it was an engagement ring. She was utterly confused and looked to Ellen for an answer. Then Jared chimed in, "Well, what do you think? Is it time to get married?"

The answer was resoundingly "Yes!" with tears flowing down her cheeks. Knowing the rhythm of their lives and anticipating Jared's next deployment, they decided to get married the very next time he had off. They were engaged on Christmas, decided for a quick nuptial by New Year's, and were wed in March. Aurora knew as a Catholic that she couldn't get married in a Catholic church, but it took a bit of convincing to come around to Jared's plan: Las Vegas. It turned out to be a fantastic fit for them. They didn't elope, but they had the classic Vegas wedding—with Elvis officiating. This plan was a huge hit with the family, and Aurora's brothers, nieces, and nephews joined them in Vegas. They shared a warm celebration with twenty-eight of their closest friends and family. Aurora's dad walked her down the aisle; her daughter was the maid of honor and gave a short speech. They ordered a small cake and had brunch for everyone. It was meaningful for them and so much fun that the guests still bring it up as their favorite wedding they've attended. With Jared, Aurora had found the spontaneity, adventure, and travel that were missing from her life. She had also found a partner who is willing to go all in.

CHAPTER

2

Brenda: "We Were Both in the Process
of Rescripting Our Lives"

At the time, Brenda was not looking for anyone to date. She was just trying to establish herself in Southern California, moving down from San Francisco after many trying years and huge life changes. The past few years had been filled will loss, grief, growth, and reimagining the future for herself. She had lost a son and a marriage and pulled herself through it by reevaluating every area of her life and changing courses to earn a master's degree in business administration. She had covered so much ground. She was ready to just have some time to settle into her new city and was content to accomplish this alone. A friend who fancied herself a matchmaker was determined to set her up. She passed Brenda's number along to Dan despite her insistence that she really wasn't on the market. He called to set up a very non-committal date one afternoon for a glass of wine, and they never stopped seeing each other after that.

Actually, after passing her number along, Dan didn't call Brenda at first. As luck would have it, he had written down the number wrong, so the call wouldn't go through. Brenda's friend asked excitedly if they had made a date yet, and Brenda sighed, "He never even called." Her friend didn't think this sounded right, knowing Dan. So she texted him and found out about the miscommunication. She called Brenda right back saying, "Don't worry. I fixed it. He's going to call right now!" Brenda still wasn't particularly excited. She was more than happy with her evening plans to relax in her pajamas. The phone rang, and she heard Dan's voice on the other side—she noticed immediately that she found it very soothing. Later, she would refer to his style of introducing himself and getting to know her as doing his "physician's interview." He was, in fact, a doctor and the director of critical care and anesthesiology at one of the local hospitals. He asked her preferences for food and wine and let her ramble on a little while, chatting. They agreed in a level-headed fashion to meet for wine in two days. Echoing each other, "Well, if we like each other, we like each other; and if we don't, we don't." They had mutual friends which made meeting feel safer on such short notice.

Hanging up the phone and reporting back to her friend, Brenda asked her why she thought they were a good match. Her friend said, "You're both educated, you both have grown kids that are out of the house, you're both professionals and you both have interest in the medical field." Brenda was skeptical about whether this was really enough to make them compatible. Or maybe she was just hesitant because she wasn't sure she was ready to date so soon after the move. But after all, it was only a glass of wine with someone she had mutual friends with.

Brenda was waiting for him at a nice seafood restaurant near her home on the island. He showed up ten minutes late in shorts and a wrinkled shirt. And Brenda thought to herself, *Oh my God, what have I gotten myself into?* She mused to herself that her professional life dealing with the medical industry really hadn't taught her about the inner workings of a hospital, but it had given her a lot of practice dealing with physicians. Like all professions, they often shared personality traits, so she figured if she could look beyond the beat-up clothes she might be able to get through a couple of hours of conversation. Besides, it was her philosophy that until someone proves differently, she wouldn't judge them. The way a man comes up and talks to you is a better indicator of whether he is a good person than the way he dresses. She knew he was a bachelor and had been through a divorce. His attire was probably a bad habit leftover from being single, and those things are changeable. When he finally explained about his clothes and arriving late for the date, it turned out that he had back-to-back meetings after he finished his shift at the hospital. Not wanting to wear scrubs after a very long day in them, he had run over to the thrift store to buy a shirt, and the rest of the outfit were back-up clothes he kept in the truck of his car. She thought that most people would get offended at a man not dressing up for a first date, but she was starting to understand the pace of his life as a doctor. Without spoiling the rest of their story, one of the first things they did after moving in together was throw out most of his clothes.

His clothes couldn't steal the show from his enthusiastic personality. She could tell he was genuinely excited to meet her. When he looked at her, his eyes went wide. They chatted over wine and realized that they had a lot in common. He ordered a bottle of Pinot Noir even though he didn't like it, because he knew it was her favorite. They had two glasses of wine each, and then he asked her if she wanted to go to dinner. Half joking, she said that she had never been to the well-known, five-star restaurant on the island, thinking it too much to ask. He was happy to go there, and she thought this was a sweet gesture, even if they did have to enjoy their fine dining complete with his shabby getup. The table was by the window, with a view of the ocean. They continued their happy conversation, and on the way out of the restaurant, all their giddy talking turned into a kiss by the fountain in the courtyard. She was surprised that it happened so soon. They walked past his car, a 1990s Toyota sedan borrowed from his dad. The engine in his car had just given out, and so he was driving this one. He asked her what kind of car he should get. She thought this was another chance to see past the superficial: She knew his job was legitimate, he had been in a long marriage, and they liked each other; so she would just have to see past the other things. She walked home alone. The afternoon was still sunny, and the neighborhood she lived in was idyllic and peaceful.

So many of us are so judgmental. We're critical. We see people online or in person and decide right away what we think of them. Maybe it's fear that keeps us saying "No way!" to potential suitors. Brenda's story shows that you should do your homework and find out what the man's life is really about and pay closer attention to how he treats you than how he looks. You might have a beat-up old book on the outside, but if you look inside, your story might unfold together.

Dan and Brenda didn't have to try very hard to find things in common. Not everyone could match her criteria, but in Dan she found someone kind and intelligent. He was the type of man she always pictured herself with: He was in medicine, mature, and reliable. Socially, they were also a match. They both enjoyed going out but were equally happy with their private home lives. They were able to talk to anyone at a social event but also protective of their alone time. They learned this by making the time to travel together while they were still not fully committed as a couple. About a month into seeing each other, he flew her out to Chicago where he was attending a conference. She thought he would dislike splitting his attention, but when she arranged to go on a unique architectural tour of the city, he jumped at the opportunity to join her. The tour allowed them to go into buildings and rooms that usually had restricted access. This seemed like a wonderful metaphor for their relationship getting deeper: They were letting each other in a bit at a time too.

It is no understatement to say that Brenda had been through a lot before meeting Dan. She lost her son to suicide when he was sixteen. When you lose a child that way, you feel you have to reevaluate every area of your life. So that's what Brenda did. She looked very closely at the mistakes she made and forgave herself. She looked at her former husband and thought about why she had chosen him and tried to understand the damage he had done to her and her children. He wasn't all bad, or she wouldn't have married him—but he had lied to her from the beginning about his marijuana use. He did much more than she thought, and the drug gave him mood swings and a dark temperament. Frustrated, she got to the point where she tried to show him how much it effected his personality by making a chart, but he wasn't willing to stop. And she wasn't willing to live in that relationship. She lost her son around the same time that her marriage ended. As a devoted mother, it's understandable that losing the things she had nurtured made her want to die herself.

She started seeing a cognitive therapist in San Francisco. She had been blessed with the resource: Amid so much loss, her therapist saw her for a year and a half for free. She didn't have any insurance, and she was learning to take care of herself. Her daughter was away at college, and Brenda relied on a circle of close friends to get her through a particularly hard Christmas. She was at the point in her life where she would have to actively choose to live. She would have to find a new purpose for her life. A friend who was an attorney said, "You're so bright. Why don't you get an MBA?" She had her undergraduate degree in business, and it appealed to her to return to school. She needed to get herself in working order first, but that became the plan. She decided to leave her day-to-day life for a while. She rented a condo from a friend in Maui and stayed there for a month. She took the opportunity to clean herself out and exercise, and when she was ready to return to normal life, she submitted her application for a master's in business administration program.

She was able to start attending in the fall with numerous scholarships and surrounded by other great, hardworking women. She didn't feel that she was fully healed, but by following her intuition and making a commitment to rebuild her life, she stumbled upon a great method to come back to herself. Unknowingly, by returning to school she was helping her brain to repair its own trauma. Using your brain heals your brain, making new pathways and connections. She found research that supported this that would eventually lead her to become involved in cognitive performance and neuro-coaching. For now, she just knew that getting through school was giving her a way forward. She had made it through the program on her own and with barely any money. Her friend suggested that she move to Southern California and keep rebuilding.

Brenda's neuro-coaching practice uses scientifically validated cognitive therapy techniques along with mindfulness. Mindfulness is the practice of returning your awareness to the present moment. It is hugely effective in combating stress. Brenda's personal coaching helps people become more creative and confident through self-reflection. She focuses on identifying and removing barriers and helping to envision positive futures for her clients so they can go after their dreams, even if past traumas are standing in the way. Her story is an excellent example of how much can be transformed if you're open to new possibilities. *It's inspiring to hear that she's had so much success healing from the past and that she can share this gift with others.*

As she was getting to know Dan, she had to confide in him about her struggles. He was comfortable with what she recounted and flattered her by saying that what he found most attractive about her was her tenacity, her strength, and her great brain. She had never been valued for these qualities before. In the back of her mind, she knew she was brilliant—growing up, she loved to visit the library and thought of herself as a geek. Sometimes, men only saw that she was a beautiful blonde and would make superficial comments to woo her. Really she was both: a gorgeous geek. With Dan she could see herself reflected the way she really wanted to feel.

Knowing that they had both been through so much and could share their pasts with each other, they decided to move in together. While walking, she noticed a little place on the island that was for rent. She texted to ask him if she should go check it out, and he replied "Yes!" right away. At this point, they had been dating for nine months. It was a great way to see if they were on the right path together. At her age, she didn't want to waste any time, and his excitement showed that he was ready to commit. Contrast this with the horror stories we've all heard and been through with the type of guy who keeps saying, "Oh yeah, maybe, maybe later, well, not now, but soon…." A woman in her fifties is likely to look at this type of guy and think, *Well, when is now? What else is going to change about our lives between now and then? What are we going to find out about each other that we don't already know?* We don't have time for these kinds of stall tactics, do we? Brenda had found the answer to her biggest question—Dan was definitely ready to make a future together.

Part of moving in together was confronting which nonmaterial things would also have to go in order for the relationship to run smoothly. Like many women, Brenda had been cheated on in the past. Dan gave no indication that he was this kind of man, but it was natural for Brenda to want to keep herself safe from exhausting entanglements and deception. He had a business partnership with a woman that he had previously dated. The business was not going well in other ways, and he wanted out. He asked Brenda for her opinion, and she absolutely insisted that this would be a good time to cut off contact with his business partner. Brenda didn't want her life to become complicated by thinking about what could happen between Dan and this other woman. In demanding he cut it off, she was being vigilant and smart. She would not allow space in their relationship for anyone else to get in the way. Some women would be afraid of making this kind of ultimatum. She had learned a lot from her painful divorce and was determined that this time, she could help create a healthy relationship. She also knew that she felt so strongly about this issue that she would rather be alone than deal with the headache and heartache infidelity could create. So she told him as much. Dan was not shocked. He already knew that Brenda was a strong, independent woman. These were her honest feelings, so it was easy for her to share them with him. He agreed to begin the process of ending the business venture the very next day.

Dan also had a firm grasp on his priorities. Before meeting Brenda, he had been apart from his ex-wife for several years. He had been married for twenty-three years, and even when the relationship stopped working well, he decided to wait until his children were grown before he would leave the marriage. Like Brenda, he wasn't particularly interested in dating—he wanted to skip right to the part where he found a quality person to commit to. They weren't discussing marriage; but they both knew that since they were monogamous, being married would be a way to easily demonstrate to other people, especially their children, that this relationship was not fleeting. It could be a way to show their values and become good role models for their children.

They had been dating a year when they decided to take a break from a cruise where Dan was giving educational talks and leave the ship to visit Paris. You might guess what follows. It's one of the most romantic cities in the world after all, but Brenda still didn't realize what was about to happen. They took the train to the Eiffel Tower and enjoyed each other's company while waiting in line. It seemed like no time passed at all. When they reached the top, he ducked away to get some champagne–engagements are common atop the tower, and they keep it fully stocked. Returning, Brenda still didn't put two and two together. They were standing at the back of the platform, and they could see the Seine River glittering beneath them and making ripples of gold light. He didn't get down on one knee. He simply asked, "Will you marry me?" and she was ecstatic to say yes. Lightheartedly, he asked if he could move a ring that he had given her that she wore on her other hand to make it become her engagement ring. She let him move the ring, still a bit shocked. It was just like a movie–people around them were getting emotional sharing in their joy and taking pictures. Six months later, they were married.

In June, they took a trip to the Cayman, just the two of them, focusing on their love. They found a woman who used to be a judge who hosted them in a picturesque cove and officiated. Dan was able to wear flip-flops and the same shorts that he wore on their first date. Brenda wore a simple white sundress. They planned to have a big event when they returned home to celebrate to make things official with their families, but for now this time was theirs alone. Despite so many struggles, Brenda had returned her life to a place that was warm and clear like the Caribbean and found someone wonderful to share it with.

CHAPTER

3

Roshan: "I Have to Tell You Something. You Are Not My Type"

Roshan has a forceful, self-assured way of walking through life. Sitting down in the crowded bar at the steakhouse in the clothes she left on after tango class, she wasn't expecting to talk to anyone, especially a man. She had sworn off men just a few days before. She even brought a book with her into the bar to prove her point.

The bar was so crowded when she entered that she figured she wouldn't find a seat. But she spotted the one seat left. When she approached, she asked the man next to it if it was taken. He had the build of a football player and replied, "It's all yours, darlin'." She was waiting to meet with her family for dinner, and this bar somehow felt safer and friendlier than others. Taking the seat next to the man, she glanced at his outfit and was a bit taken aback: He was wearing a Hawaiian shirt and a pair of shorts. She ordered a glass of wine and started to read her book. The tastelessly dressed stranger kept asking her questions, and she kept answering. She was thinking to herself that she didn't want to talk to this guy.

He asked, "What's an attractive woman like you doing here alone? Are you here with someone?"

She replied, "No, I'm not with anyone."

"Why not?" he pressed.

She replied, "Because men are stupid." What a way to kick off the first meeting with the man that would become her husband! She continued, "No offense to you, but in my experience, the men who approach me are either short and ugly or nice-looking and very drunk. Men are intimidated by me. I can't figure it out. All I know is I have a lot of confidence and I tell men the truth about how I feel and I guess they can't handle it. I'm not going to flatter men—I've decided to have nothing to do with them."

As the waiters brought Gary his food, he replied to Roshan, "Oh, really? Is that how men are with you?"

She started to be a little less bothered by his intrusions. He was eating French fries with creamy chipotle sauce, and he offered her some. She thought this was strange and kind, especially considering that sharing food off her own plate was also her custom. This peaked her interest in him, and she started to investigate him a bit, asking him questions.

Already, this was a huge contrast with prior relationships and bar experiences. At a bar, Roshan once asked a few men why they had waited until they were drunk to approach her, even though it was obvious that they had been looking her way for over an hour. They replied that she was kind of scary. *I'm scary?* she thought, rolling her eyes and thinking of how these men were acting now that they were drunk. She said to the men, "But I'm really nice! And I look good, don't I?"

One said, "That just makes it worse. You looked me straight in the eyes and weren't afraid. You didn't look away. It seems like you're perfectly attuned to your environment and you're not scared of your own shadow."

Hearing Roshan's story, it just adds to the pattern that strong, independent, self-sufficient women can and do get remarried—but it takes a strong, confident man to make it worthwhile.

Roshan didn't want to settle for anything less. She told herself that when she finished her divorce, she would like to meet the right kind of man for her. Other relationships in the past few years had been disappointing. After her first marriage, which lasted twenty-seven years, she dated Daniel for three and a half years but never wanted to marry him. He had asked her to marry him, but something made them feel incompatible. He went on trip, and when he came back, she had an intuition that the relationship was over. She questioned him about cheating, and at first he denied it. Eventually he caved, stating, "It didn't mean anything." Roshan was through dealing with the deception. He had a player lifestyle and friends to match. In some ways they were great together. He was definitely her type, suave and a bit untrustworthy. They had a pattern of breaking up and getting back together, but after this infidelity, she knew it was time to part ways for good.

What made her interactions with Gary so different? She had only just met the guy, they were eating fried food in a bar, and he was poorly dressed, so she wasn't particularly attracted. She was being herself, but also trying to keep her tendency to intimidate in check. She started talking about her interests in numerology, tarot, and astrology; and he didn't brush it off. He called the bartender over by name, and Roshan said, "Wow, you must come here often." He said not really, but clearly he did. She liked the restaurant and the good company a lot. She would have found it rude if he asked for her number, so she ended up offering hers. He had left his phone in the car, so she wrote it down on the back of his receipt. Her family had arrived, and she started to leave the bar to go to their table. Gary followed saying, "I'm going to my winery for the harvest in a couple of weeks. I'll call you to come along." Roshan just brushed this offer off lightly, assuming he wouldn't follow through. When she arrived at their table, her daughter gasped, "You didn't give him your number, did you?" Roshan said yes, but that she figured he would forget to call her and that she was going to forget about it too. That's exactly what she did.

The next morning, she received a call around eight thirty. He said, "Hi, this is Gary."

She said, "Gary who? I don't know anyone named Gary."

He replied, "Yes, you do. You gave me your number last night at the steakhouse."

Then she remembered, saying, "Oh my God, thank you for calling, but I'm very busy right now. Just give me your phone number, and I will call you back." So she wrote his number on a piece of paper on her office desk, beneath a row of other numbers to call back that day for business. She said she would call him in about twenty minutes, but the whole day passed without her thinking of it again. She was looking at her paperwork, and there was a checkmark beside each completed call for the day. There was one number remaining on the list, unchecked. She didn't recognize it, and she couldn't find it in her computer either. So she called back like she would any other business call, addressing the voice on the other end of the line with her usual formal greeting and the name of her company, apologizing for not knowing what he had called in reference to. "You called this morning, and I don't remember why…"

He sighed, "Wow, I must have made a really good impression for you to forget me so fast. This is Gary from the bar last night."

She finally remembered who he was and apologized again, saying, "Yes, I did forget you completely."

He said bluntly, "You are very honest. No wonder men don't talk to you."

She said she couldn't talk long and that she had other things that needed her attention, asking, "Well, what can I do for you?" He said he wanted to take her to dinner, and they sparred back and forth. She said she hadn't agreed to dinner, only happy hour. And anyway, she was so busy. He kept asking her times, but her schedule was full up to two weeks in the future. She said, "I'm a very busy person. That's another reason I don't want to date." He was still on the line. He wanted to know when she was available if none of the times he suggested would work. She relented, saying that she was available the next night at eight o'clock for dinner.

Arriving for the date the next night at a fine restaurant near the beach, the friction continued. She was thirty minutes late. She had called to warn him, but he didn't hear his phone. By the time she arrived, he was preparing to eat alone, standing in the restaurant bar in another Hawaiian shirt, shorts, and sandals. She gave him a hard glance thinking, *This is how he dresses for a first date?* She introduced herself too formally using her first name. He replied, "I already know who you are." And turning to the bartender, "The lady has arrived. I guess I am not eating by myself." They were seated at a table and were ten minutes into talking when Roshan interrupted, "I'm a very honest person. I just have to say before we go any further. You are not my type."

Gary was floored. "What? What is your type then? Why are you sitting here having dinner with me?"

She said, "Well, my type is usually tall and handsome, and you are that; but they're usually very fit, which you're not, and look at the way you're dressed! I don't really care since you are so confident—that gives me good feelings. I usually have a tendency toward attracting douchebags, and you don't seem like one."

Still stunned, Gary answered, "Wow, you've set the bar really high for me. You say you're honest, but actually you are excruciatingly honest. I don't know if what you're saying is a compliment or an insult." Gary was confident and strong, and the dinner continued. She helped herself to the entire calamari appetizer after squeezing lemon juice on it, which she didn't realize Gary didn't like. He loved that she wasn't shy about eating. He said he'd never seen a woman eat this much and talk this much. He wondered aloud if she worried about gaining weight.

She said, "No, I can eat what I like because I exercise a lot. You should try it." Despite their friction, the conversation went on easily for hours. They looked up, and the servers were putting up the chairs for the night, cueing them to leave. Roshan was surprised that she liked talking to him so much.

Walking outside, he took her valet check and paid for her parking. They were standing there waiting for the car to pull up, and he put his big arm around her like a watchful dog. Suddenly, she felt so protected. He pulled her closer and said, "I had so much fun. It doesn't matter if I'm not your type. Let's do this again." Not to spoil the surprise, but they continued to see each other for dinner every night until they were married. He was very insistent that she was the one for him. She once asked him why he was so insistent so early in the relationship that they get married, thinking there must be something wrong with him. He replied, "There's nothing wrong with me. I'm just very smart. All those losers that you were with let you go because they were stupid." She argued that they weren't losers. They were good people. He continued, "They were losers because they let you go. I know who you are and how valuable you are, and I'm smart. I have found the best thing that has happened in my life. I see everything I ever wanted in you. Why wouldn't I want to keep you around? You make my life complete."

Gary was honest, dependable, stable, and completely devoted to Roshan. People would ask how she managed to end up with such a great guy. Roshan said that their success relied in part on her willingness to change her perspective on the kind of men she liked. She believes that human beings have a tendency to do the same thing over and over. Sometimes we learn our lesson. Sometimes we don't. We often repeat patterns from our childhood. She finally noticed that even though all the people she had dated were good-looking and successful, they had control issues. She said that she probably carried this over from having a powerful man for a father. This pattern was hurting her until she met Gary and decided to break it. In regard to her past, she knew that there were lessons to be learned from whomever you invite into your life, but that at a certain point you have to turn away from negative partnerships. Here is how you recognize your pattern: The first person whom you see in a bar whom you're attracted to is probably a version of your old model. Your negative "type." Stop right there and ask yourself why you are attracted to them. Is it the same thing you found appealing in your exes? Be conscious. Don't be mesmerized by what's in front of you. If it seems like you're just falling into the same old cycle, don't do it. With Gary, Roshan was able to look beyond the façade when she realized how open and kind he was and how much they enjoyed talking together. Sure, his clothes gave her pause, but she thought, *Who the hell cares? If you like the person, what difference does it make what he wears?* She could continue to be comfortable with her own way of dressing. Besides, he loved the way that she dressed and having a beautiful woman on his arm, but he was not going to change his own dressing habits. It turned out that he didn't wear suits except on special occasions, but then he cleaned up well. As an executive, for years he had reserved the suit for the office and needed to be able to relax the rest of the time. In his words, "If a woman would like to go out with me, she needs to go out with me and not my clothes."

After that first long and exciting dinner together, they continued to dine together every night. The very next night, Gary wanted her to come over to his house for a cocktail before going out to eat. She wondered to herself what he was planning. He saw the expression on her face and said that she could trust him. She retorted, "I know I can trust you, and besides, if you try anything, I'll kickbox you to your nose." They rode together that night to the steakhouse, and there were flowers and champagne waiting for her on the exact seats in the bar that they had fatefully met a few nights earlier. He wanted to have dinner again the next night, but Roshan was very busy and kept pushing back the time they could meet until it was too late to go to a restaurant. So he offered to cook. On that particular night, they chatted and drank until she was a bit tipsy. When she was able to drive home, he drove behind her all the way across town, back to her place, to make sure that she was safe. A week later, they were again dining late, and he suggested that she just stay over. She agreed but said that she planned to keep her pajamas on. When she came into his room, she was wearing long polka-dotted pajama pants and a neon green top that said Princess.

"Woah, you weren't kidding." He laughed.

She said, "No hanky-panky—don't even touch me." A week later, he invited her to go see his horses in Los Angeles, and they were staying in Beverly Hills. They still had not been physical, but by then he had already asked her to marry him three times. She complained, "We haven't even been seeing each other for ninety days."

He replied, "Why does it matter? I'm not going to expire in ninety days. I'm in it for the long haul." She said those were just the rules. She liked Gary a lot, but it felt too early to be pressured into marrying, especially since she was planning only to marry once more in her life.

Returning to his place one night after dinner, he said that he couldn't do just dinners anymore and that he barely got to see her and he wanted more time with her. She said that her life was very busy, that her daughter was the first thing in her life, and that she expected to be able to focus on her career and other passions. She expected him to fit into how her life was organized the same way that he expected her to accept the way he dressed. She admitted that actually, since they had been seeing each other every night for dinner, she was already spending more time with him than with her daughter. He dropped it for a while; but as they were getting ready for bed, he said, "Well, are you going to marry me or what?"

Roshan laughed. "You don't even have a ring. A girl has to have a ring in order to say yes." So right then, at 2:00 a.m, he picked up his football ring from college and went down on one knee, asking her by her full name to marry him. She said yes unceremoniously, and he made her sleep with his ring on. In the morning, she left it on the nightstand, and he yelled after her, "You forgot your ring!"

She said, "That's not my ring!"

By now, she had a clear sign of his intentions. The proposal just needed a little revision.

They went on a trip to Hawaii and she still didn't have a real ring, but he kept asking her to set the date for their wedding. Returning home, she insisted that he talk to the jeweler that her family always used if he expected her to set the date. Gary jumped at the opportunity to move forward, he wanted a real engagement right away, but it was Christmas Eve. Roshan thought this was ridiculous timing. There's no way could he get a ring that day. Gary insisted that she call the jeweler anyway since he was her family friend. So she played along, not expecting any results, explaining to the jeweler that she was getting married and she needed a ring so she could get engaged the following day. The jeweler was shocked. He asked if her parents knew about the engagement and whether Gary had asked them for her hand. The jeweler agreed that they could come pick a ring. When they arrived, he showed Roshan some loose stones and had her pick one out and then suggested the perfect setting. It was gorgeous, but Roshan wanted to see more choices—she figured this was the last wedding ring she would wear so she wanted to be certain about it. The jeweler had the ring ready by four o'clock on Christmas Eve.

They called her parents and made reservations for all of them at 6:00 p.m. It was the same table she had sat at with her daughter the night she met Gary. Gary asked Roshan's parents for their blessing and again went down on one knee. This time she had a proper proposal to say yes to. The next morning, Christmas, Roshan asked if she could have an engagement dinner. It seemed like perfect timing to bring her whole family together. The guest list kept getting longer and longer. When he first called the steakhouse, Gary was able to convince them, as a favorite customer, to find them a last-minute reservation for four people. By the last time he called back with the guest list, they were holding a feast for thirty. Gary invited his son, and Roshan's family brought gifts of champagne and flowers. Her parents were a bit insulted that they weren't informed that this was a formal engagement party. Roshan's traditional Persian father was upset that he hadn't known to bring a gift for the engagement of his oldest child. So Roshan said, "Don't worry. We'll just have another party then." In the spring they had a larger party and were married in the fall. They had a peacock-themed wedding, enjoying every chance to celebrate their union with a bit of flare.

All throughout their courtship, Roshan had clear signs of Gary's intentions and affection. She had mentioned once that her dream car was a blue Corvette. Then on the first birthday that they spent together as a couple, there it was in his garage, waiting for her surrounded by balloons. He joined her in tango lessons and never expected her to give up any of the activities that she enjoyed. They worked to align their goals for the future—though Gary's ideal was to spend half the year travelling, Roshan wanted to continue to live in the same city as her family. When they met, Roshan had already selected a house for herself. She showed it to Gary, and he said, "Are you sure this is the house you want to live in? Because I don't want to move you twice." They hadn't been dating long at that point, but she thought if she ended up with him, then she didn't need this house all to herself. She followed her gut and stopped escrow. Later, they decided to buy a house together.

Sometimes all the joy of a couple and their new life can have an effect on existing friendships. Roshan's best friend saw all that she was acquiring, both in terms of a stable, reliable relationship and lifestyle changes, and became jealous. Up until then, Roshan and Geena had been inseparable. Roshan also knew that Geena had some devious tendencies. She was the kind of woman who directed male attention to herself even if someone was hitting on one of her friends first. Geena already had everything a girl could want: She was strong and beautiful and had money, but she was unhappy. She made a habit of surrounding herself with friends of lower status to feel better about herself. Roshan was the only friend she treated as an equal, but things changed when Gary entered the picture. Once, when Gary and Roshan invited Geena to lunch, she brought several attractive girlfriends along. The women focused their attention on Gary, and Roshan felt it was blatant attempt to get him away from her. One of the women had a window cleaning business and gave her card to Gary for use at his company. Between all of the ladies at lunch, Gary couldn't focus on Roshan, and it looked like Geena enjoyed watching this manipulative situation unfold. Back at the house, Roshan brought up how wrong his actions had been, but he didn't see the harm in the lunch. Roshan fumed, and Gary told her that she couldn't tell him what to do. She promptly got up and packed a small suitcase she kept at his place with all her belongings and declared, "You're not the man for me. At this moment, we're never speaking again. Lose my number." She carried her suitcase down to the car, got in, and sat down. Running after her, he grabbed the car door and would not let go. They had only been dating a month, but they had been seeing each other every day. She told him that he couldn't speak to her for two days. After that she would be calm enough to talk. He destroyed the girl's phone number and waited for Roshan to talk to him again. Roshan knew herself well and knew what she needed when she was angry. They learned very early in their relationship how to ride out conflict.

Geena and Roshan were still friends by the time of the engagement party, but Geena was still looking for ways to spoil the harmony. Since Roshan danced tango, she wanted to include some dancing at the engagement party. She asked Gary if he would enjoy this, and he said humbly that he would prefer to see her dancing at her fullest instead of working with his beginner's moves. He said it would be better if she danced with her teacher and that it would be fun to watch. At the party, they did just that, but Geena took it as a sign of infidelity and started making a scene. She said she didn't want to be Roshan's friend anymore since she had made her engagement about another man, trying to take the moral high ground to hide her jealousy. She refused to attend the wedding, which crushed Roshan. It's especially sad when women are cruel to each other when they should be sharing in each other's happiness.

Geena's response to Roshan's happiness was negative, but it was outweighed by all the messages of support and hope that she received. After she was married, she received messages on social media from women of all ages, who said that they had lost hope that they were ever going to find a partner but that Roshan's success had returned their hope. Roshan assured them that the main thing she had done to find the relationship was to be herself. In the past, she had tried to change herself to match her partner, and it hadn't worked. This time, she respected herself so her partner could respect her back. Well, maybe there was also a bit of dumb luck involved: on the first night they met, that seat next to Gary was the only one open in the crowded bar; otherwise she probably wouldn't have given him a chance.

Roshan's husband provided me with some special insights into what drew him to Roshan: *"I married her because she's funny, sincere, and brutally honest with very little filter between thoughts and voice, and she loves me very much. I wasn't looking for anyone, but then she breezed into my life, and I've never been happier."*

CHAPTER

4

Jenna: "Do Women Like to Swim in Circles?"

She's the type of woman who has always been sought after. She knew that in some ways men are easy—they're easy to figure out when the main thing is that they want you. So Jenna found it strangely refreshing that Harry had a difficult personality. The sparks between them at first were ones of friction. They both had dominant, independent personalities; and although immediately attracted to each other, their early relationship was marked by emotional negotiation, jockeying for position and eventually molding each other into partnership. They both had to change their behavior in some ways to feel mutual respect and a sense of security that would allow them to rely on each other and invest emotionally.

Speaking with Jenna, her sharp and contemporary personal style is supported by clear and forceful word choices. She's what most men would consider a stunner. At six foot and three inches and always in elegant heels, figure-flattering clothes, and neatly edgy blond bob haircut, she naturally draws attention when she enters a room. It's obvious that's she's worked to maintain her body and her looks, but nothing about her is flashy or ostentatious. Her statuesque physical appearance is filled with inner strength. She said that she was raised to believe she could do anything she wanted to do. The strong males in her family shared some of their strength with her. Her father honored her independence, and her grandfather echoed this philosophy with dating advice, "Play the field, Jenna. Don't settle down too quickly." Even so, her approach to relationships has always been committal—she's been in one long-term relationship after another, almost back-to-back since her teens. She hasn't really spent any time single in her adult life. Now, in her third marriage, with Harry, she attributes her success in many areas of her life to her positive attitude.

Her philosophy is to remain baggage-free. She said this is an inner choice—that basically, she accepts change very quickly. When things aren't working in her professional or romantic life, it may take some time to realize she needs to leave the situation—but once the realization has occurred, she moves on very quickly. She chooses to look after herself by abandoning any resentment or bitterness that might follow her to the next opportunity. She admits that she doesn't know how she acquired this attitude—but it's obvious from hearing her story that she's had plenty of moments in her life when she had to shift gears, so perhaps it's all about sticking to the attitude you want to embody. You could say practice makes perfect. It takes work to maintain a positive outlook and learn to accept change.

The major conflict in her first marriage was that she shared too many aspects of her life with her husband. They owned a printing and manufacturing business in the sporting goods industry. Sharing a domestic life and business was not the best fit for Jenna's independent personality. She's also a woman who likes to be in control of her own life. Conflict arose when her husband started mismanaging the financial affairs of the business without informing her. She said she hasn't had any bad relationships—that's why she has no baggage. Sometimes it's important to get out before resentment seeps in. If she has the foresight, she actively chooses what she invests her time in and makes major changes when something is no longer serving her. But she's not perfect. She feels her way through life like the rest of us. On the eve of her second wedding day, she had a feeling in the pit of her stomach that it was a negative relationship. Her fiancé was erratic when he drank. So close to the event, she figured the wedding was already in the works, and she should just go through with it. After her second marriage ended, her friend took a very cynical view, taunting her that she would never get married again. In fact, this friend is still single, while Jenna has found a new relationship.

It's not unusual to see evidence of women perpetuating the stereotype of the spinster or old maid. In loneliness and insecurity, we might even lash out at one another, making predictions about our friend's love lives. What Jenna's story shows is that this is useless thinking. Jenna is particularly passionate about this topic saying, "What is it? Do women just like to wallow? Do they like to swim in circles?" We mused together about the different patterns that seem to appear in women's dating lives. Some get out of a long marriage and have a trial and error period and then find a relationship that sticks. Some marry much too young, and it stops working a decade later. Or they wait to marry until they are well into what would be considered, in negative terms, spinsterhood; and it sticks. We decided that, in fact, there are no patterns when it comes to remarriage. With Jenna, all her relationships except her second marriage were long-term, committed situations. It isn't necessarily the "right" way—it's just what worked for her, to constantly throw the negative off her back and keep moving.

Jenna met her third husband through friends. She was still married to her second husband but going through divorce proceedings. At first, she slowed their getting together, even though the chemistry was immediately obvious. She wanted to take a conscious pause between relationships. She had seen that her judgment was off in going through with the second marriage and was concerned that if she jumped right into a new relationship, guilt and the other feelings she was still processing would poison the well of newfound love. She wanted to take a moment to discern how she had contributed to her toxic previous relationship. In some ways, she felt that her second husband had brought unresolved negativity from a previous marriage into theirs, so she was being extra careful not to mirror this behavior. She also wanted to assure a clean break by waiting to get involved with someone else until her divorce was finalized. Jenna carries herself as a high-value person. She has her own career and knew that if nothing happened right away in the relationship department or if this attraction to Harry didn't lead to anything, she'd rather spend time with friends than date random men. She ended up pausing for about six months.

She might have appreciated a bit more time; but the day after her divorce paperwork went through, her coworker said, "Guess who's coming to the party tonight?" It was his tall neighbor Harry, whom he had been trying to set her up with. She knew the spark was already there. Months ago she had scoffed, "I don't want to date your nerdy neighbor" thinking that if someone is trying to set you up on blind date with someone, they must have horns or something. Recently, she had seen him through the office window a few times, and her interest had been piqued.

Harry and Jenna started dating. Going out to dinner frequently, they discovered they had a great deal in common—from the Danish heritage that gave them their height to a love of architecture, films, and travel. It also became immediately apparent that they both wanted control. Part of Harry's maneuvering for the lead included a bit of emotional manipulation—he was still dating younger women that were easy for him to discard and acting like he didn't have to invest in emotional connection to get what he wanted. Jenna knew right away that this playboy attitude was not the stuff of mutual respect. She wanted a deeper connection and always held him accountable for respecting her, telling him point-blank on several occasions that this is what she wanted. She felt she didn't have time for dealing with a superficial situation or one in which she was being used. At the same time, the friction between them created an attractive challenge. She could have walked away, but she decided instead that it was her job to help Harry grow from someone who sought disposable relationships out of insecurity into someone who could maintain a real relationship.

Harry had been single for twenty years, and it had taken its toll. His attitude came off as inadvertently self-serving. He would forget dates and not call to apologize. He had a very reserved, cool demeanor in general, but when he started sharing the details of a stressful situation, he couldn't stop talking and would over-share. He was still carrying a lot of pain and resentment from his first marriage. He was used to being alone, and this kind of solitude affected how he interacted with others. He confessed once to feelings of isolation and disconnection saying, "I live in two worlds: the hard construction industry and the other world—where am I supposed to be at home?" He acted like he expected to own parts of Jenna but not all of her, whatever was convenient or suited his mood. Jenna stood her ground. She called him out on unacceptable behavior. She recounted to me a backhanded compliment he made when they were struggling to define their relationship. He said, "You're the first woman I've been with who's my age who doesn't remind me of my mother." The relationship continued to deepen as they sorted out the issue of mutual respect. Jenna learned from all these negotiations "that you have to let them know what you want and be clear about it."

As Jenna got to know Harry's family, his issue of over-sharing became a problem. They were initially thrilled to have her as a potential new family member, seeing in her the possibility of a stable, mature relationship for Harry. Harry shared with them that they had been fighting, and the family suddenly turned on her. Conflicts also appeared regarding his impending retirement. Harry was generous with his money and took good care of his family, but they were concerned about sharing their son's resources with a possible new wife. Harry was feeling similar pressure from a business partner who wanted more control over shared finances. New and important alliances form in marriage. Harry's reaction to this situation was a pivotal moment for proving his commitment and building stability for him and Jenna. When Jenna shared her concerns over the infighting that was occurring, he unequivocally took her side, telling her that if they were to marry, she would always come first. After all the squabbling between the two of them, this laid solid ground to start to build a future together. If the person you're with sticks by you in the face of an external conflict, that's all that matters.

They were engaged and eloped to Hawaii a year later. The tone of their relationship changed immediately after they were married. Gauging Jenna's impeccable personal style and independent thinking, Harry had her select her own ring. They were joined by a small group of friends including Harry's children. The fire between them had been fortified into something more stable. The emotional tone between them shifted. It turned out that the security of total commitment soothed Harry's difficult personality.

It was the start of a new marriage, but they brought with them their maturity and aspects of their past. The hardest thing for Jenna was to recognize when she needed to let go of control and let Harry take the lead. She maintained her ability to be clear about her expectations. Jenna had her own home, but decided to move into Harry's house before they were married, "Because you've got to try them out." She said that when they were deciding on which of their houses to move into together, she agreed to move into his only if he would allow her to remodel the whole thing. It sounds a bit like a metaphor for their relationship, and their abilities give each other a structure for the future while helping each other change. Jenna gets to bring a bit of herself and her aesthetic to the space while symbolically working to integrate their lives. The house is full of dark wood paneling, which is not her style, but she felt it was important in the remodel to respond to existing elements and allow it to be a hodgepodge of the things they love. When I met with her and heard her story, they had been married for eight months. They are still getting to know each other, and I bet that house is still being rearranged.

In Jenna's case, the power struggle between her and Harry signaled their passion for each other but also became an obstacle. In the end, she had to learn to compromise while still making her needs clear. What is one obstacle you have encountered in a successful or unsuccessful relationship? Identifying the difference between meaningful obstacles that lead to growth and absolute deal breakers is one of the keys to building a successful marriage.

CHAPTER

5

Tricia: "We Don't Do Anything like This on My Home Planet"

Tricia hadn't seen Dane since he was a child. He was such a wild thing then, jumping off furniture, filled with energy, so different and free. As he grew into a young man, his mother became fed up with his behavior and sent him back to New Orleans to live with his uncle and start at Tricia's high school. Now at sixteen, they had just pulled in, Tricia ran out to the driveway to say hello, and there was a strange feeling of electricity between them. She was tall and extremely skinny with big, thick glasses and long straight hair, and it was the first time she felt attractive. He was looking at her with a gaze that said, "Where did you come from?"

He was only a month older than her, and their families were old friends. They had grown up together, but she hadn't seen him in years. Now he was attending her high school, and the bond between them made them feel and act just like family. She routinely introduced him to her girlfriends as dating prospects. He even ended up going to prom with her best friend. As high school ended, they started spending more and more time together, going on double dates with their own love interests. In New Orleans, the bars don't close, so she would go to dance and he would go to shoot pool. He would play for drinks and get so many that he couldn't drink them all, so he'd give them to her. She would be out dancing, and they would compare notes on who they found attractive in the bar, whispering to each other, "Oh, look at that guy!" or "Here comes that girl. Go talk to her!" They were best friends. They did everything together, just with other partners. When they were out dancing, if a good song came on, they would spring to their feet and go dance to it together. Whomever they were dating at the time would get upset at being excluded and at the special connection between them. Somehow, Tricia never realized it herself. She had no idea why her boyfriends were getting offended—it never occurred to her that Dane was anything but a best friend or that their friendship could become something else.

They both got engaged young: They were both eighteen, Tricia's boyfriend was twenty, and Dane's girlfriend was sixteen. Tricia received a mailer saying that she had won a trip to a resort in Hot Springs, Arkansas—free accommodation, meals, and other amenities. It was the beginning of the time-share phenomenon, so they didn't recognize what it was. They were just kids looking to have a good time, so they took the trip. When they arrived, they were given a golf cart to use for the weekend and attended a sales pitch. The salesman took one look at them and said, "Are any of you twenty-one? Oh no, well just enjoy your weekend." So they took off and had a great time. That's the sort of adventure they liked to have together. Their engagements didn't last long. Dane left New Orleans to join the Navy so he wouldn't have to follow through with his fiancé. Soon after, Tricia felt she was too young to get married, so she broke off her engagement too. The first person she called after the breakup was Dane. He said she needed to get away and invited her to visit him in Memphis where he was training. He promised to set her up with a friend of his who was cute. Nothing ever came of this setup except a few letters back and forth and Tricia getting to take her first ride on a plane to go visit. With their lives unfolding apart from each other, they grew in different directions. Dane was stationed out in California. When he got married, she didn't want to attend. Tricia met her first husband, and Dane wasn't at her wedding either.

The way they communicated changed. They would stick to Christmas cards, with pictures of their kids and spouses and brief updates. Tricia was living in Houston, and he only visited her once in many years. In the same span of time, she only visited him and his family in California once too. Her feelings for him never crossed the line of thinking and behaving like they were anything but high school friends, but something was going on below the surface. Occasionally she would dream about him. It made her wonder how he made it into her dream life so many years later. It only happened every so often, maybe ten times in twenty-five years, but it was memorable. She would wake up sighing, "Aaah, it was only a dream, but that was pretty good," smiling to herself. It was strange but welcome. She didn't keep track of what was going on with him in the interim, but it turned out that his marriage had fallen apart. Meanwhile, her marriage was barely holding together—she and her husband were counting down time until their kids were out of high school and they could confront the realities of getting divorced.

The same uncle whom Dane had lived with in his teens was having a sixty-fifth birthday in New Orleans, and it was set up to be a reunion of sorts. Dane flew out for the festivities. Tricia was getting ready to drive to the hall which was an hour from her house. Her husband agreed to go but demanded to take his own car because he wasn't planning to stay long. In many ways they were already acting separate. When Tricia arrived and saw Dane, she was amazed. There was still a palpable spark between them, except this time it seemed more substantial. Her husband left as soon as he felt he had put in the minimum time, and a group of her friends and family decided to go dancing after the party. Dancing had always been one of her favorite activities and something that filled her with new energy. The spark she felt earlier in the evening with Dane was becoming more of a magnetic attraction. They kept gravitating toward each other on the dance floor and sitting next to each other. He was dancing with other people, and she was too until things drew to a close around 3:00 a.m. Everyone was making arrangements for sharing rides home. Tricia's brother and her friends were there, but she accepted a ride home from Dane instead.

The extra time to spend together was too much to refuse. When they got in the car, he turned to her and said, "I have to know."

"Know what?" she replied.

He said, "I just have to know. I have to kiss you."

"What!?" she exclaimed, totally stunned.

They drove awhile and pulled off the road, and Dane said, "Get out of the car."

She refused, still stunned but smiling wide. He insisted until she followed through. He kissed her, and that was it. She was lost. From that moment forward, she was hell bent on spending as much time as she could with Dane. Nothing mattered but the sensation of their connection. She didn't worry about whether it made financial sense or not or other practical considerations. There was only one path she was willing to take forward, and that was toward him.

After that dynamite kiss, she didn't even know if he would call again. He called from a rest stop as he drove away from New Orleans the next day. It knocked her off her feet that this was actually happening. She kept thinking maybe she was totally nuts and this was not really moving forward, but they ended up talking several times a day for the next ten weeks. They couldn't get enough of each other, but there was a lot of geographical distance between them that they had to figure out how to traverse. He lived in California, and she had returned to living in New Orleans. He was separated from his wife, and she started to proceed along the same lines with her husband. Her husband had already been moved by his oil company out to Houston after Hurricane Katrina shook New Orleans. When he moved, he didn't even ask her to go. She knew she wouldn't have gone anyway. It seemed like Tricia and Dane were free to proceed with their relationship. After a few months apart, they finally took a trip together. They traveled to see each other for two years, back and forth, often meeting while he was traveling for business. In this time, her divorce was finalized.

It took those two years for her to be really ready to tell everyone about the relationship and leave New Orleans. She didn't get the chance to consciously choose the moment of explaining things to her family and friends—it snuck up on her. Dane was visiting for Mardi Gras, and they went to the French Quarter. Her daughter was there with a friend from college. They were at the world-famous Pat O'Briens, and the young girls had gone off to the lady's room. While they were gone, Tricia and Dane snuck a kiss. Standing in the doorway across the room from them, the roommate noticed the kiss first and turned to Tricia's daughter exclaiming, "Did you just see what I just saw?" Tricia's daughter, of course, knew Dane, but she only ever thought of him as Tricia's friend from when she was in high school. Tricia's daughter replied, "Oh my God, they kissed! I did see it! Oh no, oh no." Tricia's divorce was final by this point, but no one knew she was seeing Dane. A couple of days later, Tricia's daughter asked her about the kiss, thinking she would deny it. But instead, Tricia started laughing. She knew it was time to tell the rest of her family. Her son did not take the news well; he was still hoping his parents would get back together. Blending families with adult children can be really hard. There's just no good time for kids to see their parents separate and start new lives with other people.

It was time for Tricia to make arrangements to move to California. She was the owner of a commercial real estate company, and she sold it in order to move. She had already sold the big house she had lived in with her husband. She rented her condo out. She had lived in New Orleans most of her life. To be with Dane she was leaving behind a lot of history, her mom, and her brother; but she had evidence that it was time. Someone in the family had sent her a box of old photos. Digging through, she found a picture of her with Dane when they were sixteen. They were beaming and seemed so natural together. Looking closely at the photograph, they weren't touching—they were very close, but there was about an inch of space between them. When she saw this photo, she finally understood that the connection between them was very real and had been building all this time. Their spark reached all the way back to their youth. She was ready to leave everyone behind, get in the car, and start her new life in California with Dane.

Starting to draw their lives together, it took a long time to make things peaceful with their children. Her kids used their southern manners to act like they were supportive of their mom, while his kids made her out to be the villain that had ended their parent's marriage. Tricia mused that she's not sure which kids had the better strategy for coping. She also believes that it's typical of all kids who go through divorce, even adult ones, to secretly want their parents to get back together. Any new mate their parents start seeing would be greeted as obstacle. His girls were fifteen and eighteen when she joined him in California. Her children were eighteen and twenty-one. In the beginning, they couldn't even do family events together. His kids just wouldn't accept her. One Christmas, because they refused to come over when she was home, Dane loaded up their motorhome with all the kids' presents and met them somewhere without Tricia for a mobile holiday. The initial defiance toward accepting Tricia ran so deep that when she suggested to one of Dane's daughters that she was bright and attending college was a good idea, she decided right there on the spot not to go. She apologized years later to Tricia, realizing it wasn't her fault, but in the moment, it was very painful. Another time, the kids asked Dane to go on a boating trip; and when he arrived, his ex-wife was there. They had invited her in hopes of getting their parents to reunite.

By the time that they got married, five years into living together in California, the kids had barely softened their attitude toward Tricia. They admitted that being at the wedding was really tough for them, but they went along with it. Tricia really just wanted to have a fun event with her family. Dane's uncle was still in New Orleans, so they decided to take a cruise out of the city. Her best friends who still lived there acted as her bridesmaids, and she was able to right a wrong from her first marriage. She asked her sister to also be one of her bridesmaids. She is her only sibling, but they were not close as children. Tricia's first marriage was very small with just a maid of honor and best man, so she didn't include her sister. She always regretted that decision and was happy to have a second chance twenty-five years later. Dane's mother was there and was very accepting of the situation even if she wasn't crazy about it. She had known Tricia since she was a little kid. Tricia was a little worried about how the kids might act on the cruise since they were still quite angry, but they didn't cause any disruptions. They threw a bridal shower, and then the boat embarked for Cozumel on a three-day, four-night trip. Tricia and Dane were married on the beach in Cozumel. They didn't spend the night there. They wanted to keep it short and sweet. They returned to New Orleans and later traveled to Hawaii for their honeymoon. They had another reception for their California friends once they were back home, and it looked like the kids were on their way to a little bit of acceptance. By the time I met with Tricia to hear her story, things had changed a lot. It's been five years since she married Dane, and she now has a very rewarding relationship with Dane's daughters. She often goes to dinner and shopping with the younger daughter, and his oldest now works as her assistant. Hiring her to do her bookkeeping means Tricia trusts her with her most intimate financial matters.

The strangest thing about their marriage was that Tricia had literally found the man of her dreams. She expected everything else after that to be roses, but she quickly realized that real life is much more complicated and demanding. It wasn't just the kids who were a struggle. The relationship had an entirely different mood than her last one, and blending in with his friends proved impossible. Her first marriage was placid. Like a lot of women, she longed for more passion. The problem with passion, which they had plenty of, is that it meant ups and downs. The bad times were intensely bad, and they both had triggers left over from the wounds of past marriages that they had to learn to navigate. Though there were plenty of intensely positive moments too, starting a new relationship after a certain age felt like walking through a minefield. It's important for women to know that not every story is just simply happily ever after. Tricia figured out that a second marriage was a chance at a new beginning, but sometimes it also felt like coming in at the end of a three-hour movie. She had given up everything known and stable in her life to embrace this fateful love affair, so she had to be willing to change if it was going to grow in positive ways.

They say that hindsight is 20/20. *Tricia found something invaluable with Dane, but she said it would have been much easier to tackle all of the obstacles coming her way if she had known just how difficult starting over can be.* She moved to her new husband's city and would be far away from what was familiar to her, trying to integrate with his friends and family. She felt like more than half the burden to compromise fell rightly on her.

Would you relocate for a second chance?

How much of your life would expect to stay the same?

Just because they grew up together did not mean that they had similar customs or lifestyles. They were on the same path when they were eighteen, but then their lives completely diverged. It was hard to mesh all the experiences that had happened in the meantime. His friends and interests were completely different than hers. She was used to more sophisticated settings and southern manners. Dane's life was California casual. His friends preferred to take some beers out to the sand dunes and ride dune buggies. She felt like she was riding along through a trip to another planet. The Imperial Dunes really do look like outer space, but the behavior of his friends was even more alien. The first time they went out to the desert, they stayed in tents. Tricia was amazed and didn't see the appeal. They were going to a place where there were no restaurants, no shops, and no showers. She made no complaints, but her quiet hesitation made Dane's friends think she was "uppity." It was a theme with them. Going to visit his best friends at the house where they had been roommates, he just walked in instead of knocking on the door. So Tricia stood in the doorway. She could see two of the female roommates stretched out watching TV, and she waited for them to invite her in. They never did. It was this moment that made her realize that she was walking into a life that was completely different than her old one. She decided to strive to build her own friend group and activities outside of the relationship and also start finding mutual friends and activities for them to start fresh with.

It's common for people to think that the only thing you really need to find to have a happy marriage is the perfect person. This just isn't true. There's a lot more to contend with. Finding the person is not the end of the journey. It's the beginning of a new one together. When you're not in your twenties anymore, you carry with you your history and financial position. Remarrying might not even feel like starting over. Tricia said, "You can't build a new life from scratch when you remarry; but if you're aware of how the new partnership affects others, especially the children, who don't get the benefit of having a say in what happens, you can move forward with integrity." Be prepared to be welcoming and understanding when you can. Be prepared to explain your financial thoughts and lifestyle choices to your new spouse.

Tricia and Dane's goal for their ten-year anniversary is to go on a riverboat cruise in Europe. In the meantime, they're playing pickle ball two or three times a week. It's an intense game that she calls "old people's tennis." The ball is a Wiffle ball, so you can put as much force as you want behind it and no one is going to get hurt. It's a fantastic way to blow off steam. She pulls her hair away from her face, and at the end of a match, the ends are dripping with sweat. It's a full-body workout that is gentle on the joints, and it's a lot like dancing, which was always a hit with Dane and Tricia. You can tell a lot about these two from their body language. Looking at another picture from their youth, side-by-side with one from their wedding, their stance is the same, but they have grown into themselves and embraced the passionate romance. In the photos, they look into each other's eyes adoringly, and you know it's the real thing.

Tricia said, "The heart is going to take whom it wants. When the person comes within tackling distance, it's just going to happen."

CHAPTER

6

Shelley: "You Don't Know Me Well Enough to Marry Me"

The stories I have heard from women who have remarried in their fifties and sixties have been overwhelmingly positive. As I've collected the stories, I've become firmer in my belief that there really is hope for a happy second chance. I would also like to acknowledge that there's value in being single. Each woman in this book has spent a certain amount of time alone, reassessing her life—that time may have been brief, or it may have spanned over many years. In most cases there is an element of choice involved in being single. We all recognize that to start over, sometimes you need to work on yourself, set your life in order, and get to know your needs very well. What happens if you meet your second husband and it turns out you really did prefer the single life? That's what Shelley's story is about. I offer it not as a discouragement but to give the full picture of the reality of remarriage. There's a positive side to almost every relationship, and in Shelley's case, she might have been able to be more content with her marriage had she known her beau longer or instead stuck to her guns about enjoying the single life.

Shelley was single for decades. She spent about thirty-four years building her career and learning to plan and execute the life she desired for herself. She was married for eight-and-a-half years in her twenties to a man she met in college before they went their separate ways. Now she's an editor, and she works for a nonprofit that does educational research. About a year ago, she became office manager, and there are thirty-eight people who work at the office and about ten who work off-site around the country, all of whom she oversees. Some women are intent on finding a new husband and they really look, but Shelley just didn't care for the idea. In her thirties she was having a lot of fun instead, dating a lot of nice people and going out to plenty of nice dinners. She was devastated for about a year after her divorce, but then she just got on with her life. She loved travelling, and in her forties she took a leave of absence from work and went to Europe for six months by herself. She enrolled in the University of Salamanca in Spain and took a semester of Spanish and spent her weekends travelling around Spain. After the semester was over, she went to Switzerland for a time. She made short trips to Italy and France. She especially enjoyed Paris. Her life was fulfilling without a husband—she knew that when you live alone, you have to consciously plan your life and think about what you're going to do. When you're married, you already have a million things to do, and certain parts of the future are laid out by your husband and kids. When you're single, you have to consciously accomplish the things that give you pleasure, and Shelley was a master of doing just this.

It wasn't just her independent nature that made her predisposed to the single life. She grew up as an only child and had a tendency to be self-centered. She never wanted kids and didn't really feel she had much motherly instinct. Growing up, everything had always been focused on her. It's not that it made her spoiled, but it created a very specific family dynamic that molded her as she grew up. She started to think the world revolved around her until she got to college and had to share a dorm room and realized, "Oh my goodness, I am not the center of the universe." She was raised in New Jersey but picked

Arizona for college because her dad always wanted to move there. Her parents also moved to Arizona around the time that she started school. They hated the New Jersey winters and found the fact that in Southern Arizona it would be 80 degrees in January very appealing. So even this move seemed to keep her as the center of attention, but that's when her independence really started to kick in. That independent attitude was what sustained her through three decades of single life. Until she met Joey.

Shelley had a girlfriend who kept asking her to go dancing with a big group of friends. They went every week, and they wanted to include her. Shelley is not much of dancer, so she hesitated to say yes. Her friend persisted, and eventually they went out. Shelley was introduced to the whole group, and Joey was among them. They danced on the afternoons and the weekends, mostly at street fairs to live music. Shelley was talking to many of the folks in the group, and Joey asked her to dance. She became self-conscious and told him that she wasn't a very good dancer, and he said, "Well, take a look at everybody out there—how are they doing? Do you see any really great dancers?" She thought this was sort of funny and very true, and it made her feel less intimidated. So they danced and talked. She found out they had certain things in common: They're both from big cities back east, they belong to the same political party, and they both have master's degrees. It felt like they had quite a bit in common. She didn't know at the time, but he is twelve years older than her. It didn't show that night—he seemed much younger and certainly light on his feet while dancing.

After the night of the street fair and their synchronous conversation, she kept running into him around town as she was going about her daily life. She would bump into him at Seaport Village or Little Italy. She went out again with the group of dancing friends and saw him then too. Her girlfriend kept pressing her to come out more—Shelley had been on her own for a long time, and her friend figured she needed some encouragement to meet new men. After running into Joey a few times, he asked her for her email address. He started sending her emails that didn't say much—just quick notes to invite her out wherever the dancing group was going. It was all fairly innocuous, and when he saw her in person, he would ask her to dance. But everyone danced with everyone in this group of friends. She had no reason to assume he was interested in her. They were friends for about six months before that changed. She wasn't looking for someone to date, let alone a husband. She truly preferred being single. Somehow they ended up on a formal date at a private social club, and though they had been out to eat before with their now mutual friends, this felt completely different. After that, they dined together consistently, and it finally sunk in that this guy was interested in her.

She really enjoyed his company. He's very smart and well-educated and knows a lot about things that interest her. Everyone kept saying, "Oh, how nice you *finally* found someone." People were so happy for her she figured she better start buying into the excitement. Inside, she thought that people were assuming that if you're alone you can't possibly be happy and that you're just masking sadness if you act like you are. Shelley knew herself well, and although she was more than willing to give this relationship a try, she didn't realize how long it takes to really get to know someone and let them get to know you. They dated seriously for only about six months before the idea of getting married was brought up. It probably wasn't long enough for her to acclimate to this new life, but she felt he was a genuine and interesting person and decided to be with him.

He brought up the idea of marriage one night while they were at his house watching a movie. He started talking about his marriage to his first wife, who had passed several years prior. He made the casual inference, "Wouldn't it be nice if we got married too?" and she replied, "You don't know me well enough to marry me." He supposed she was right, and she continued, "And I probably don't know you well enough to marry you either." They had only known each other for about eight months at this point, so they dropped the subject for a while, but it was clear that he wanted to get married and the topic was never out of conversation for long. He had been married to his first wife for forty-eight years, and he liked being married. In the seven-year period since she had passed away, he had been single and actively going out with friends, but he was very lonely during that period. He was used to having someone to share his life with day and night since he and his first wife were inseparable. Here was Shelley, whom he enjoyed spending time with but who was a very different kind of partner, independent to the extreme and not looking for a marriage.

She suspected that he was going to formally ask her to marry him. She spent many evenings at his house—she worked nearby and would often stop in for a couple of hours to wait out rush hour traffic before driving home. He texted her all the time to invite her over, but she wasn't always available—she maintained her social life with her girlfriends. She knew they were an item after a couple of months of going to lunch together on their own. Most days they communicated somehow—whether over email or text. He had only mentioned marriage in passing so far, but she knew he was going to ask her. She could just feel the vibe. She just didn't know when. Whenever they were watching a movie together and a guy got down on his knees to propose, Joey would say, "Do guys still do that? It's so corny." Nonetheless, his daughter helped him plan a romantic surprise for the proposal. They went to a nice restaurant, and there were flowers and sparkling wine waiting for her on the table. She thought they were just going out to lunch, but this was something more. He didn't get down on one knee, but he still wanted a dramatic setting. He knew what kind of ring she would like from a previous shopping trip. Even though she had known for some time that the proposal would happen, she was so taken aback by the actual words that she couldn't answer at first. It had, after all, been several decades since she was married. She just kept repeating, "Oh my God, oh my God, oh my God," in place of a reply. He was sitting there anxiously waiting for her to answer properly, and it was clear how nervous he was about possible rejection. She finally returned to her usual composure and said yes.

They were married three-and-a-half months later, and the event was very small. At first, they thought about having a larger wedding, but the list of people to invite kept getting longer and longer. She would think, *Do I need to invite the people whom I work with? Are people going to feel bad if I don't invite them?* It can become very hard to figure out how to invite some but not all of the people you would like to see on your wedding day. He wanted to include his whole family, inviting folks from Ohio, and the list continued to get longer. As they visited restaurants to hold the event, Shelley finally realized, "I've already had the big, fancy wedding when I was young with a big white dress and veil and all the hoopla." She didn't need her second marriage to contain these elements, so they decided to just do a small ceremony with immediate family. They liked to visit Laguna Beach together, so they held it there and stayed near the water for nine days for their honeymoon.

Suddenly, Shelley was married after many years of being single, and in truth, she wasn't at all sure if she liked it. Shelley had a very good life before she was married, and she's not afraid to be alone. To her, time spent single didn't even feel like "alone time." She was ful- filled by friends, travelling, and work and never succumbed to lone- liness. Not everyone feels this way about constructing their life on their own, but Shelley did. She's both outgoing and naturally solitary. Getting married to Joey began a difficult transition in her life. All signs while they were dating pointed to her need for independence, but once they were wed, he expected that they would be together all the time. It felt like he was asking her to drop her former life and accept a whole new one. She made it very clear while they were dat- ing that she expected to go to work until she couldn't and that she liked being part of the working world. She couldn't imagine what she would do all day otherwise. He accepted that she would con- tinue to work full-time but had a harder time going along with her social schedule. She wanted to continue to do things with her friends without him. They would argue, and this would make her miss her old life even more. She didn't have any children and her parents had passed away, so over the years she made her friends her priority. They felt as close as family to her, and losing precious time with them felt like too large of a demand. Her social life became an ongoing argument between them. She was always home by 8:30 p.m., and they would usually be able to have dinner when she arrived. Still, Joey wasn't very good at being alone.

Things evened out between them over time, but occasionally, their lifestyle differences are still a point of contention. She admits she let him steamroll her into a life she might not have been ready for. She calls herself a feminist but then wonders to herself what kind of feminist lets a man convince her to marry him. For all her independence, his personality is more intense than hers, and he naturally takes the upper hand. Comparing Shelley's story to my own, I remember when my husband and I were dating. He said to me that he knew his relationship with his ex-wife had big problems when she wouldn't eat dinner with him. She wouldn't even sit down. He would be eating alone, wondering why he was even in the relationship. I knew because he commented about it several times. I was going to be expected to spend meals with him, but eating dinner without my husband wouldn't have occurred to me anyway. Unlike Shelley and Joey, we had the benefit of dating longer before becoming engaged.

Joey was longing for more time together and interdependence. In an ironic and sad twist of fate, he became ill with cancer, and his sickness required Shelley to be at home at all times. They were married just four short months when he was diagnosed. It was a major shock to both of them since there was no reason to expect that he was sick. It was discovered during a routine physical that he had both colon and prostate cancer. The process of becoming a married couple became a process of coming to terms with his illness and treating it. He became so sick that Shelley didn't think he would make it. It was almost like their honeymoon faded into a nightmare. She used up all her saved vacation time and a hundred hours of sick leave to stay home and be his nurse. Overnight, she went from wife to caretaker. Everything changed. He did recover. He has healed, but he remains very weak and she still takes on extra responsibilities to keep him safe and sound. She worried about losing her job, but when she returned they promoted her. Shelley is happy that she retained her connection to the world outside their marriage and happy that her husband has recovered, but there is still much to mend between them.

Shelley's advice to women is: "I know there's a lot of women out there who don't want to be alone and are actively looking for someone, but you have to be careful not to go from the frying pan into the fire, just to not be alone. What if the marriage ends up worse than being single?"

CHAPTER

7

Laura: "The Lord Never Removed from Me the Desire to Be Married"

Meeting with Laura, she spoke with measured, assured words. The story of how she remarried is a story about her Christian faith. She truly feels she has been blessed, and after hearing her story, it's easy to agree with her. Many challenges tested her ability to stay true to her values and trust in God, but she made it through. Laura said, "God never removed from me the desire to be married. So I knew that meant that he had something for me, somewhere out there, but I was going to be very careful and very intentional with any relationships." After the struggles of her first marriage and the twelve years of healing and reimagining her life that followed, she was able to embrace a relationship with John from a position of wholeness.

Her late husband was bipolar. He was a sweet husband and father with many talents, but sometimes it seemed like half of him was out of control. It was hard for Laura to tell if this also meant that he wasn't trying to control his mood swings. When mental illness becomes a destructive part of a relationship, the fine line between what is sickness and what is a person's individual responsibility becomes hard to distinguish. After many tumultuous years, Laura lost her husband to suicide. It was a gut-wrenching loss, but Laura consoled herself that at least her husband was finally at peace after decades of instability. She had always been the one to keep the ship from sinking. In hard times she believed in rolling up her sleeves and doing whatever work was necessary to push through and raise the kids. They raised five children together—four boys and a daughter. At the time of her husband's death, the youngest son was preparing to leave for college. Their daughter was just starting high school as a special needs student. Laura found a way to turn this extra challenge into another blessing—she believed that her daughter's condition gave her the "gift of purpose." She had to get up every morning and keep their lives on track, leaving little time for pulling the covers over her head and wallowing.

Through the grief and years of recovery, she relied on her Christian faith to keep her steady. She became twice as invested in her personal relationship with God. Sometimes she wondered what the bigger plan was, but she knew it would take time to move on to the next chapter in her life and that even though she knew she wanted to find another husband, she would never be willing to adjust her value system just to align with someone else's. She was surprised to be pursued by a number of men, but she was being judicial with the grieving process: It took her two years to take off her wedding ring, and she focused her energy on taking care of family finances and her daughter. She wanted to be sure that she had built a solid and stable foundation for the future, especially since there had been so little stability during her late husband's illness. Still, she saw the value in her first marriage. Her son told her that he thought they had a "very loving but troubled home."

She was fortunate to have created a solid financial foundation through timely investments that kept them comfortable. They had always lived beneath their means and saved. Her husband left a huge amount of debt that was the result of many scattered business ventures ranging from jewelry design to real estate. Laura spent some time untangling their joint ventures and returned to work. She had worked on political campaigns since college, and by the time her youngest child was in kindergarten, she had signed on to manage her first campaign. Working gave her an outlet and a sense of purpose and control. It kept her strong and confident to experience her own successes outside of the struggles of marital dysfunction. Though she had stepped back when her husband's condition worsened, the political world now welcomed her back with open arms. She was once again blessed to have found a career path that allowed her to do what she loved, and the money followed.

Four years after her husband's death, a number of things had become balanced in her life, and it seemed she was poised for the next phase. Her youngest daughter was able to go to college, thanks to extra resources and assistance on campus. This left the house empty. Laura signed on for the next political cycle, but she felt she had done everything there was to do locally and didn't want to move to DC. She felt God's voice was telling her it was finally time to just sit still, no more pushing through life's requirements and taking care of others—it was time to just let things be. This panicked her. She had always just kept swimming no matter how choppy the waters became. She felt like it was a season in her life when she was forced to dream. She asked herself questions like "If you could do anything, what's the life you would choose?" It was agonizing at first. She simply didn't know how to be still. She was used to a full calendar and a full house. So she became even more involved in church and let her faith guide the way. She started visualizing a new life and praying for it to be built.

As she was building a new life in her mind, she asked God what qualities she should have as a good wife and what to look for in a husband. She started to be very specific about her criteria, starting out with the most important qualities for a match. Besides the obvious necessity of sharing her faith, first and foremost, she wanted to be with someone she respected and enjoyed spending time with.

This sounds simple, but it took many years to find someone who merited her attention. The men she met either had conflicting values or weren't her intellectual match. Sometimes, on dates, she felt that the conversations were so unstimulating that she had to recite the bill of rights in her head just to stay awake. The world tried to convince her that at fifty-eight she was too old and too chubby to find a great husband and that her heavy emotional baggage from her past made her unworthy. She knew this was a false identity and chose instead to listen to God's assurance that she was of value. She was seeing a grief counselor around the time that she started dating again, and it provided a great opportunity to deal with other issues from her past. She was taking the time to sort everything out so she would be ready to start fresh if she met someone right for her. Her therapist suggested that she try online dating. Her therapist knew that there would be no guaranteed results but suggested that Laura might benefit from sitting down and filling out the questionnaires on the site. It turned out to be a very helpful exercise to answer the questions about her specific lifestyle and values and what she expected from a partner. Online dating also ended up providing enough material for about ten years of stand-up comedy.

One comically bad date was spent with an aggressive commodities broker from Orange County, California. He was attractive, his personality was dynamic, and he had a high-power profession—everything the world says a woman should want. They were the same age and had common interests in restaurants and theater, so it seemed like they would have lots to talk about. She felt he was too insistent about wanting to meet, but she finally gave in to a date for happy hour near the beach. She wanted to make sure it would be easy to walk away if she needed to. It turned out that they hadn't talked enough before they met for Laura to really get a sense of whether or not their values were aligned. When she arrived at the restaurant, it was still sunny out, but he had arrived before her and already finished three-fourths of a bottle of wine by himself. He talked about how he was bored with work, so he wasn't taking good care of people's investments. He told her about how his kids had no direction in their lives and how several of them were on drugs. He said that his philosophy right now was that he just wanted to fall in love and make the rest of his world go away. She was seeing red flags all over the place, but when he asked her to continue their conversation walking on the beach, she obliged. They had been walking for about ten minutes when she asked him how long he had been on the dating site. He said he had only been using it for a couple of weeks, which surprised her. So she asked, "So this is your first date?" He replied, "No, I've been on nine dates in four days." Then she knew that was it. They were a terrible match. She said, "I don't sense that there's enough here to move forward, so I'm going to take a step back" and started to walk off the beach. He pleaded with her that they were perfect with each other; and when that didn't work, he became indignant, saying, "Women don't know what they want. You're all teases." Laura just kept walking away, got in her car, and drove away laughing. If she wasn't convinced that what God promises is true, she probably would have become discouraged or bitter. She chose to believe that good things were in her future.

With experiences like this, she would use the dating site for a while, decide it was too ridiculous, and turn it off. She had always teased one of her colleagues for having the site as a sponsor on his political radio show, sharing her horror stories with him and his wife. One evening at a fundraiser in their home, they were laughing about it again, and Laura said that this time she was really swearing off the sites. Her friend argued that it was a valuable way for people to connect. He assured her that the site had changed a great deal since she was last on it and wanted her to promise to try it one more time. She had been single for over a decade, and her friend was encouraging—he wouldn't let her off the hook until she gave in.

As luck would have it, this one last unwilling tour of the dating site was when she met John. She was amazed that he possessed both of the qualities she prized the most: She respected him and enjoyed talking to him. Her faith-based system had been so strong and specific that she recognized immediately that this was a man she could spend her life with. His messages and answers stood out—finally, someone whom she felt like she wasn't just going through the motions with when chatting. They had been talking online for some time and she loved the depth of his intellect and how their values mirrored each other, but what if there was no chemistry or he was different in person? They discovered that they had mutual friends, ones she held in high esteem, and that's when she felt he was trustworthy enough to meet. They met at an Italian restaurant, he reached out to shake her hand, and the moment that they touched she felt energy shoot up her arm. He had brought her a single long-stemmed yellow rose. It was clear to her that this was the best first date of her life and the only one that had her whispering to herself as she left, "Please call me. Please call me. Please call me." Dinner and conversation had lasted three-and-a-half hours. Spontaneously, halfway through dinner he stopped mid-sentence and said, "You are really beautiful." It was genuine and kind, not at all meant to get something from her. It made her feel giddy and young. She was smitten, but would he call?

She received an email the next morning. She was already telling all her friends about her great first date. She was so excited to relay something other than another online dating horror story. He called her that night and asked her out for the following weekend. She was always receptive and never the aggressor. That was the pattern with them. She learned through their discussions that they were both looking for the same godly marriage, that their personalities were completely complimentary, and that they were both looking for a relationship from a position of wholeness. Neither of them was asking anyone to fix a broken part of them. John had been divorced for ten years, and his kids were his focus. He had sacrificed dating for them, which told Laura a lot about his character. He didn't give serious consideration to finding a new wife until his youngest finished high school. He was a mechanical engineer, an instructor, and the vice president of a laser research marketing and development company. Laura loved how his personality combined science geek and cowboy. He admired her quick-witted involvement with politics. They shared the same Christian faith which was essential. Their priorities were the same, and it looked like they were headed in the same direction. You can't say that that unless women wait twelve years to remarry, it won't happen—but in Laura's case, the time on her own had helped her become emotionally whole and healthy.

Six weeks after they started dating, he was scheduled to spend a week in Thailand overseeing the opening of a factory. He called her twice a day from Thailand, and they shared some increasingly intimate conversations. They talked at length about their desires and dreams. Perhaps being half a world away made it easier to talk about the things that really mattered to them and become more personal and transparent. It was a week that transformed their relationship. He spoke logically and rationally about the way things were progressing between them. He said he liked the direction they were headed in but needed more time to be sure. She already knew he was the one.

Laura really felt that here at last was her gift from God and that there was no way it would have happened so perfectly, otherwise. She was in awe of God's timing too and how he found her all the components she needed in a husband and at the best time. It had taken so much faith to wait it out. She survived many tempting opportunities in the past to be with men that would have required her to shift her values. She would think to herself, *Maybe if I just bend a little, I can make this work*, but she always ended up deciding to stick to her guns. It was especially difficult for her as an independent, self-sufficient woman to watch and wait. In other areas of her life, she was used to being proactive: If she saw a problem, she would just go out and fix it. This time she knew she had to practice being receptive. There were times before she met John when she would be so impatient that she would be praying and wringing her fists at God saying, "Do you know how long this is taking?" and then she would laugh to herself, "Of course he knows." Her kids wanted her to be safe and not make a bad choice, but they worried that she was being so selective that she wouldn't ever find someone. Her faith would always return stronger than ever. She would say to them, "No, God has something for me." Here at last it looked like it was coming true.

They were about eight months into dating, and John assured her in his characteristically rational style that it wasn't good timing to get married. His company had just been acquired, and he was the key transition person. He would be buried in work for the next six months. Laura accepted this, things were steady between them, and she felt privileged to be beside him as he entered the peak of his career. Meanwhile, John was planning a proposal. To keep it secret, he never asked her ring size. Instead he used his engineer's mind to make a guess, gathering information by comparing the size of the fingers of the ladies who worked in his office. The Friday night before Christmas, he took her back to where they enjoyed their first date, saying, "Things have been so crazy at work. Let's just get a casual dinner, put our feet up, get a bottle of wine, and debrief for the week"; so it seemed like nothing out of the ordinary was about to happen. They arrived at the restaurant, and he had arranged for a dozen yellow roses to be waiting for her at the table. This reminded her of their first date. He had a few other surprises up his sleeve. As they were ordering, he said, "I'm really loving where things are with us, and I know once you decide that you're peaceful about us, we can move forward." Laura was confused. She did feel at ease in this relationship. She possessed real clarity about what she wanted and why—and this was it. Besides, wasn't he the one who said he needed time to focus on work? He pressed her again with the same statement in slightly different words. And a third time he teased, "Not until you're sure." She didn't know that this was both a sweet trick to build up the surprise and his way of getting her assurance that she was ready to get married again. She was starting to get upset at the repetitive questioning when he stood up. Laura was about to yell "Where are you going?" when he got down on one knee and proposed. The restaurant erupted in applause. She was so caught off guard she was shaking.

He nailed the size of the engagement ring exactly. The surprises kept coming. Three waiters walked out of the kitchen each carrying a vase filled with a dozen red roses. As the waiters paraded through the restaurant, she just hung her head and cried tears of joy. To her, it seemed like only a moment had passed, but in reality, it had been closer to a full minute. John leaned and whispered, "You haven't given me an answer yet." She managed to say yes and embrace him, but she spent the rest of the evening so completely stunned she couldn't stop exclaiming her surprise.

John planned the engagement's many amazements, but Laura planned the wedding. She set out to make a brief and heartfelt occasion with cake and champagne for toasts; but when she described this to John, he said, "But when do we dance?" She replied, "I guess we're doing a full-blown reception then." The wedding was attended by one hundred people, with full dinner, dancing, and a band. They held it at a clubhouse that sat on the edge of a picturesque manmade lake. His son was the best man, and two of her sons who are pastors co-officiated. This was a really special sign of family involvement and commitment to her faith. She was given away by her late husband's younger brother, another very positive sign of all the healing that had occurred within herself and her family. She was freed from the brokenness of her first marriage, and things were stabilized for everyone involved. There was no resentment in either family that would keep them from moving forward together. The solid foundation she had spent the last decade working to establish was firmly in place and echoed in all the love around her, a true celebration of faith and family.

Yellow and red roses were a recurring part of Laura and John's romance. In many cultures, plants have been given specific symbolic meanings. Flowers were given a secret language all their own so that lovers could communicate by sending specific bouquets or depicting certain blossoms in art. This practice was especially popular in the Renaissance and Victorian England. Gifts of flowers were seen as coded messages that the recipient could decipher with a special dictionary. The meanings of flowers vary depending on time and era, but the poetic power of roses is enduring. *Yellow roses are commonly taken to mean friendship, while red roses communicate true love and passion.*

Two years into their marriage, it's still astounding how much they have in common. The differences in their upbringings are very minor, and they enjoy nostalgic comparisons of their time in high school. John is four years younger than Laura, and she teases that he's the baby of the two of them only when she notices that they listened to different music in high school. The minor age gap comes down to this: She remembers when the Beatles broke up, and he only remembers that they were a band in past tense. He might have been listening to the same song on the radio in junior high while he was babysitting that she heard played at her prom. In adulthood, their politics align, and Laura's political resumé was one of the things that attracted him to her. It proved that she not only voted a certain way but was passionate enough to get involved and savvy enough to figure out how to get paid for it. One of the best nights they've spent together since getting married was election night. She was done with her part of the political process and was sitting at home with her laptop watching Secretary of State returns, with the commentary playing on TV. John was excited to see politics unfold from the inside as Laura was able to predict and narrate what would happen next. As she watched the way the election was trending, she would call out in advance what would be said next on screen. John would turn and say, "How did you do that?" Laura said that "Men respond to women who admire and appreciate them. It spurs them on and draws them deeper to you than anything external. When you have genuine admiration for them, they just double down in their devotions to you." It looks like in her second marriage, this admiration and devotion goes both ways. She's at the point in her political career where she would rather be at home watching the returns. She's a state delegate, but she rarely goes to conventions anymore. She's thrilled to have someone to spend her evenings with, relaxing in pajamas and just seeing how things unfold.

Laura's advice: "Don't be discouraged: You can have one night to have a bubble bath pity party when things get hard, but you've got to get up the next morning and start again. Do the work to heal and to be ready and worthy."

CHAPTER

8

Lisa: "That Guy over There Looks Kind of Cute"

Often, successful, happy men want to get married too. It's not unusual. If anything, women learn to be alright on their own as they grow older. The women I have met who have remarried weren't desperate to find someone. Sometimes they knew it was the right time for them and that they enjoyed life more with a partner and went looking. Sometimes things just lined up. The women I've spoken with are resilient, strong, and independent, though all with very different personalities, lifestyles, and needs. Women might think or feel that there's a pattern and that older men only want to date younger women, but this simply isn't true. I think women do a lot of work themselves to spread this idea. Stories like Lisa's disprove this notion. If older men only looked for younger women, they might end up with someone who still has kids in the house or a fulltime career that doesn't allow them much time together. This might be ideal for some couples, but for others, meeting later in life affords the opportunity to travel and enjoy retirement together. Lisa certainly wasn't looking for someone, although she had the charisma to never be without a date for long. The man she met turned out to be romantic and focused on fidelity—when I met with her, they had been married for twelve years.

Lisa was married when she was younger, she had three children, raised them, and went on with her life. She met Mitch when she was fifty-three, and they dated a year and a half, and then they got married. She was a professional at the time she met him and had just retired from working as a leasing manager within the healthcare industry. They have always kept their money separate. Lisa has no idea what his checking account looks like. He has no idea what hers looks like. They take turns paying for dinners out. The house is in her name, and he decided to move in with her, so he gives a certain amount every month to maintain the house. She likes it this way. They live in an ideal location, and she's been enjoying her home for twenty-five years.

A critical part of many of the stories of remarriage I have heard is that the man has to be the instigator. He has to be in all the way, or else don't waste your time. That has nothing to do with age. There is a certain art to signaling availability that works well in some situations, and that's what helped Lisa. Though it wasn't entirely her idea, a friend at a Christmas party pressed her to mingle more and identify the men she might be interested in. After a couple of hours at the party, Lisa was ready to leave. She really didn't want to drink anymore before having to drive home. Her friend insisted that she stay a bit longer. They argued back and forth. Lisa was really ready to leave. Her friend said, "No! You have to meet someone here," and dragged her over to a group of guys standing across the room. She pressed, "There's gotta be someone here that you want to meet." So, just to appease her, Lisa said, "That guy over there looks kinda cute," pointing to Mitch. Her friend dragged her over to the group of men by the refreshment table, embarrassing the heck out of her, saying, "My girlfriend thinks you're cute" and then she walked away, leaving Lisa there, not quite knowing what to do. Mitch was a gentleman about it, and they started talking. The conversation was getting interesting, so they went outside to talk where it wasn't so noisy. When she was ready to leave the party, he walked her to her car, gave her a kiss on the cheek, and said, "Can I call you?" She said yes, and he called her the very next day.

He called to ask when they could get together that week. She said she was only available on Monday and Friday. His joke after their first date was always, "I took Monday, and I definitely got Friday." Their first date was extravagant. They went to one of the finest restaurants in town, and he brought her two-dozen yellow roses. This might have been taken as a show of his romantic spirit, but Lisa had to wonder if maybe he was acting a little too hungry. Her impulse was to hold back a little. The gesture just seemed way over the top. As she got to know him better, she realized that this kind of display was just part of his personality. He is a wonderful, demonstrative partner and handsome to top it off. Mitch is retired from army intel and was working as an army contractor. He had a full-time job. He didn't have any children and never really wanted any. Her children were grown and off living their own lives. This made it possible for them to focus on each other as they started their relationship. It eliminated the possible point of contention that appears when children see their parents dating someone new. Lisa also knew she had her own career and she could support herself and buy her own clothes and cars. She had no need to attach to someone else just for financial support or a sense of security. This made them a very good match.

After their first date, he immediately asked if he could take her out Friday night. After that, it was a regular pattern to meet two or three nights a week and go out together. He was always outgoing and personable, leading them to have many charming evenings. He pursued her, but it also felt like they were establishing a comfortable rhythm of being together and they shared the pleasure of moving the relationship forward. She's the one that gave clear and ladylike signals that she was available; but he's the one that really initiated the relationship by asking for her number, walking her to her car, and calling her the next day. They both preferred this traditional power dynamic. He seemed to know a lot sooner than she did that they were establishing a long-term relationship. She had been single for so long, and she was used to taking her time to get to know someone. It took about six to eight months before she realized that they had the potential to go the long run. Dating is amazingly different over the age of fifty. Sometimes one or both partners could have health issues. Hopefully you're making more money than you did in your twenties, so you're more established. That also means that you're more set to have it your way, personality wise and you have more non-negotiables. While dating, it's not uncommon to feel that it would be fine if the relationship doesn't work out because there are aspects of your life that will always take priority. If someone you're dating can't accommodate this, you're more likely to wish them well and move on. This was another reason Lisa was slow to get attached. She was stronger and less insecure than her younger self. She knew how to take care of herself. So many of us grow up being told, "Your goal is to get married." That's life. So when examining the chance to remarry, it's nice to look at it with a fresh, more mature perspective based on what you actually need from a relationship and whether the man you are marrying is a solid, dependable match.

A word on red flags:

Lisa said that she has found that if a man hasn't been married, had children, or had a similar responsibility, he has a hard time sharing; and I couldn't agree more. I always warn women: Don't even date a man who has never been married or had kids, if you're looking for commitment, because that adjustment would be too hard for them to make. It's possible that they never really learned to share or they're just not compatible that way. It's not that they're bad people—but just imagine: If you had spent your whole adult life spending your money on yourself, pampering yourself, and fitting a date in here and there when you're in the mood, that and getting married are two entirely different things. At a young age it's one thing, but a man over forty who has never been married, that's a major red flag.

Mitch had been married before. He was married to one of his ex-wives for ten years, and she had three girls. He was commitment-minded and had actually been married three times. One of the only major conflicts that arose early in their relationship was finding out that he had concealed the fact that he had been married not twice, but three times. He was self-conscious about seeming like he was always getting married. After discovering this, he was in the doghouse for a long time. It was a serious issue because it shook the foundation of trust they were building. She didn't understand why telling her was a big deal. He was afraid that it would change her opinion of him, but that wasn't the point—trust was. She should have been allowed that knowledge. She wanted to know all of the important things about the person that she was committed to.

A year after they had met, they celebrated the anniversary of their first date, and he asked her to marry him. There are so few romantic men, but Mitch is one of them. Early in their relationship, Lisa even encouraged him to write a blog about it to help other men get a clue. He set the proposal up with the restaurant. After they had ordered appetizers, the waiter came out with a covered plate. When she opened it, Lisa found the words "Will you marry me?" written in icing and the engagement ring sitting on a butter dish. The second she opened the cover, he got down on one knee. She said yes right away. She laughs that the one thing she would have changed about the proposal is that he invited a bunch of friends to also dine at the restaurant that night. What if she had said no? He figured if she rejected him, he'd have them there to party and drink with, but the proposal had been a success so they stayed and enjoyed the many congratulations of their friends.

A month later, the romantic gestures continued. They were watching Casablanca on TV, and Mitch said, "Have you ever been to Paris?" She had been there once, but only for a few hours—she had blown through once with a gentleman she was dating; they had lunch and just moved on with their travels. So Mitch replied, "Then you've never really been!" Three weeks later, he surprised her with two tickets for a week in Paris. Lisa said, "There aren't enough words to describe the feeling of the trip. How wonderful it was."

Six months later, they were married. They had a party at the same house where they had met. Her friend offered it for their reception. They enjoyed the company of one hundred friends and family. They had just returned home from a luxury cruise to Greece. The captain of the ship married them just outside of Mykonos, and they invited a bunch of their closest "never met you before" friends from the cruise for an instant celebration. Getting married at sea is not a legal venture—it was symbolic and ceremonial for them. At home, they had already been to city hall and followed the proceedings with a lovely moment in a hillside park with arboretums and incredible view of the city. It was misting rain that day, and they left the park to go to lunch with several close friends at one of the most famous restaurants in town. At the very top of a tall building, the view from Mr. A's was equally gorgeous. So in a way they had a threefold wedding. They just never got tired of celebrating.

Over a decade into being remarried, Mitch travels quite a bit for work, but for Lisa it's a fabulous excuse to both enjoy her independence and visit him in exotic locales. He was in Abu Dhabi for three years, but they Skyped every day. She saw him in person every three months. Their relationship is built on the solid ground of secure personalities and kept lively and warm by Mitch's knack for sweeping Lisa off her feet.

Lisa's advice: *Don't be so picky. Be confident.* "They're not perfect and we're not. Don't exclude good, honest men because they have a bald head or a little bit of a gut. Don't compromise your values but see if he really is a wonderful person beyond outward appearance. Take care of yourself and get out there. You don't have to wear makeup all the time but do a little more than just expecting it to come to you. Make an effort. Taking care of yourself will give you more confidence, and nothing is more attractive than confidence."

CHAPTER

9

Judy: "We Should Just Start Over"

Judy was invited to a Super Bowl party, and when she walked in, she found a bunch of her friends and only a few people that she didn't know. James was one of the people she didn't recognize. There was only one seat left that night, so she sat down next to him and they started talking. Of course, they weren't supposed to be talking because the Super Bowl was on, but they were quickly engrossed by their similarities. Polite small talk like "Where did you grow up?" revealed that they went to the same high school. Both were in their seventies and had long moved from the place they grew up in, but here they were, old classmates. Most of the people at the party were married, and Judy assumed that James' wife was around somewhere. She just wanted to talk to him as a new friend. So they had both gone to North High in Phoenix. She asked him what year he graduated, and he got mixed up and remembered the year his wife graduated, which was while Judy was there. She was very confused why they had missed each other back then. He had spent the last two years of high school elsewhere, but Judy realized that she and his wife had been cheerleaders together. It was eerie. James told her that his wife had died two years ago. She hadn't seen her since high school, and yet they had so many mutual friends on the West Coast. They must have been invited to many of the same parties but just barely missed each other; otherwise, Judy would have recognized her. James was beginning to get excited that their social circles were so connected and started to ask, "Do you know so and so?" They continued to connect while everyone around them was probably thinking, *Will you guys shut up?* hoping to focus on the football game.

What made the situation even stranger was that Judy had been separated from her husband for two years and hadn't told any of her friends. They had been married for thirty years. So the people at the party didn't know her status, and she hadn't seen them in a long time. They were a bit gossipy, and she felt more comfortable keeping it to herself. She hadn't officially divorced her husband yet, and she put off saying anything about it. So her friends started to wonder why she was sitting there, married in their eyes, giving so much attention to James. An hour or so went by, and finally one of her girlfriends yelled from the kitchen, "Hey, Judy, where's your husband?" Judy was mortified. She went up to them and said, "Well, it's a long story." As they were cleaning up at the end of the party, she explained to the girls that she had been separated from her husband for two years. She just hadn't told anyone. They were already living separately too. She didn't want them to think that she was just sitting there, flirting with some guy while her husband was who knows where. There was actually a lot of competition for James's attention at that party, but it didn't register at the time. Looking back, she realized that there were at least five other single women at that party, and he was the only single man. They were all old friends, but Judy was sure that the one that yelled out "Where's your husband?" had designs on James. The other women whispered in the kitchen that James was financially successful, but Judy didn't know anything about him and that wasn't what sparked her interest in him. It was strange that everyone knew him but her. She was embarrassed about what her friend yelled, but she still decided to give him her business card, inviting him to come visit her at her shop some time. She walked away from the party thinking, *He'll never call me now.*

Later in their courtship, she asked James if he heard what was insinuated about her at the party, and he said that he didn't even hear. Still, it took him weeks to get up the nerve to visit her shop. Real estate was her primary business for many years, but when it became too feast or famine, she decided to open an antique shop selling furniture that was upcycled and refinished. It assured her a steady cash flow, and she had been in business for twenty years. After meeting James, she would go to work wondering if he would stop by; but as the days went by she thought, *Okay, that's that.* Apparently, he checked with his friends, and they told him she was married. He must have checked again and got his story straight because he finally decided to visit her. She recognized him right away when he walked in. She gave him a big, welcoming hug. Later on, he told her that gesture made all the difference. "I probably would not have asked you out if not for that hug. I was just too scared. It took me two weeks to even get up the courage to come over to your store. It made me feel so much better that you were warm and open with me. I was so nervous." He wasn't used to dating at all, and it's educational to women reading this to remember that men do get nervous. They can be hesitant since they don't want to get turned down. This was a big step for James. He had been married all his life. They chatted for a while, and he casually said, "I'll give you a call. Maybe we can go out to lunch or something."

Again, she waited a couple of weeks before hearing from him, making her doubt their connection. Then he did call and set up a lunch date at the fish market right on the wharf. The seafood was fresh, but the atmosphere was about as casual as it gets, not exactly first date material in her eyes. They ate, and the conversation was pleasant enough, and that was it—she went home. It was such a quick, nonchalant hour that she left wondering if there was any reason to see him again. Their second date was a bit better—a proper date at a steakhouse a week later. Then things became much more regular between them. Judy admits that dating at their age was a little awkward. Both of them spent most of their lives with spouses. She was only a couple of years younger than him, and trying to figure out courtship rituals in their seventies proved difficult. The conversation between them was comfortable at least—he loves to talk so Judy would just wind him up and let him go. His story was inspiring: He came from nothing and worked hard to achieve what he has. He was lucky in his younger days to meet the owner of a warehouse club store who helped him build a future for himself. He started out as a box boy and became CEO after many years of commitment. They went out almost every night. Their conversations became less cursory and more romantic.

Immediately after dating, James wanted Judy to move in with him. She replied, "No, I'm not going to move in with you unless we're married." He was surprised and asked why. She answered, "You have grandchildren. I have grandchildren. You have children. I know that for younger generations it's no big deal, my grandkids live with their boyfriends, and some are not ever going to get married. That's okay for them, but we're older. You have little grandkids, and it's hard when grandma has died. Had grandma been divorced it might be easier, but it's such a sensitive area for someone to just move in." He understood, but he didn't like it. He wasn't looking to get married. He figured his marriage was over. He just wanted to spend more time with Judy. He continued to tell her that he wanted her to move in with him, and she continued to draw the same line: no cohabitation before marriage. So then he figured that getting married was inevitable, working "So when are we getting married?" into conversation. Judy said, "Wait a minute—you have to ask me first." He replied, "I do?" and she insisted, "Yeah, you do." He finally got a clue.

Even though they were operating under her stipulations, she felt a little pushed into it. James had his mind set on becoming engaged. They were shopping at the mall, and they stopped at the jeweler's and he started asking her which rings she liked. He decided right then to save himself a trip and purchased her engagement ring on the spot as well as a new wedding band for himself. He was efficient, but he threw a little romance in—he went down on one knee right there in the store the second the rings were purchased and asked her to marry him. The girls in the shop were impressed and started cooing. James had a bad knee, so this was a grand gesture. Judy laughs about his rapid proposal now, but that day she accepted it on the spot. They had spoken about the possibility of him proposing earlier in the week, and he had tried to confirm in advance that she would say yes if he proposed. He was a bit embarrassed to be asking and wanted to stave off rejection at all costs. This casual couch proposal was concluded with "Great. You can move in this weekend." He was really pushing, but she insisted on a real proposal at least, which is how they ended up at the jeweler's. It was all still a bit of a surprise— she was trying to play the game where you coyly show your beau the jewelry you prefer so they can sneak back for it later, but James had escalated the process. Of course, she said yes.

Probably both James and I thought it was not going to happen again for us at this age. It was very scary for me to get a divorce. But when you're not happy and you're lonely in your marriage, you start to think it can't be any worse to be on your own. I did think it would be nice to meet someone, but I wasn't even divorced yet when I happened to meet James. Before that, I thought, Why bother? *Sometimes I would try to figure out how to meet someone, and it was difficult. I tried online dating, but the men on the site were low quality. The main thing I would say to women is that sometimes you're actually trying too hard. At the point I met James, it just happened. I think that is often the case.*

Their relationship had come to the point of commitment very quickly. They had been dating only six months when he proposed. James just wanted to get back into the rhythms of married life. He had been miserable on his own. Then their wedding was delayed by an unforeseen tragedy. They planned their wedding for early in the New Year, but they received a terrible call on New Year's Eve. They were in Palm Springs for a party and had guests staying with them when they found out that one of James's daughters had died. Kat was not in good health and was recovering from a series of surgeries. It appeared that she accidentally took too much medication. What made the loss even harder was that Judy had known Kat before she even met James. Kat was a regular customer at her store, and when they realized that Judy was dating her father, they were both delighted. What a small world filled with a strange turn of events.

Once the wedding was delayed, they started to discuss more seriously the prospect of moving in together. James had a house in the eastern county that he wanted Judy to share with him. There were a couple of issues with this plan: It was far from her work, and he hadn't changed a thing since his wife died. A woman does not want to move into a home with another woman's décor, and what's more, it felt too much like time had stopped and preserved a shrine to his dearly deceased. It was clear to see that James hadn't reclaimed the space for his own life. Still, Judy didn't want to be disrespectful. It did make sense that if they were going to start a new life together, they should also start over with a house, and it was something they could afford to do. A lot of men look at remarriage as an opportunity to replace the little Mrs. with a new one. Judy was her own person and didn't want to live immersed in old memories. She knew that wasn't the healthy choice for either of them. She also figured it would be strange for James's kids and grandkids to see the house changed just a bit but with a new wife in it, and she was trying her best to be sensitive to the situation. They finally found a house to buy together. She really had to stick to her guns; otherwise, he would have insisted that she just move in and pick up where his first wife left off.

Financial considerations also stood in the way of getting married. The process of ironing out the prenup had become tedious and, at times, hurtful. Over a certain age, it is common for this to happen. It might seem like once you've found the right man and decided to get married, everything else will be peaches and cream, but many people go through the lengthy challenge of the prenuptial agreement. It can get ugly. Other people who aren't directly involved might say things, the lawyers, the kids, and friends; and either party might get offended. These people don't know you, and if they did, they would probably see that there are other reasons for getting married besides money. In Judy's case, this was definitely true. She wasn't after James's money or his kids' inheritances, but he wanted to keep their finances completely separate. This made Judy feel she would be unprotected should something happen to James. They even broke up a couple of times over the disagreement but were never apart long. She eventually grew tired of the conflict and compromised. She was sure that if they were both in the same financial bracket, it wouldn't have been much of an issue. She has friends who got married later in life with similar economic situations who easily merged their finances so that everything they create after they are married is mutual property. However, this sort of equal score rarely happens when you're older.

They were finally ready to get hitched. James said right away, "Let's not get married here. Let's just elope to Hawaii." Though they both had children, it didn't make financial sense to bring everyone out to the islands. James is a very private person, and it appealed to him to have their ceremony all to themselves. Judy's first wedding was the usual big event, so she had no desire the second time around to walk down the aisle in a white dress and veil. By the time they were married, they had known each other for a year, and the wedding had been delayed twice.

They've only been married a year, but they are planning to go on a fifteen-day cruise to the Panama Canal for their second anniversary. It's already been scheduled. They're going with another couple: friends who were her friends and his friends before they became *their* friends. It has been fantastic to join their lives because they didn't have to make new friends—almost everyone they loved were already friends to both of them.

"Sometimes things are just meant to be, and they happen whenever they're supposed to. I would ask friends to set me up or try other ways to meet someone, and it didn't work. The whole time, James was already in the middle of my social circle. It just had to line up."

CHAPTER

10

Vera: "I've Never Felt This Way about Anybody. I Have to Tell You That I'm Attracted to You"

People ask me if there are women whom I know who have never been married and are in their fifties. Most of the women whom I have met while discussing remarriage have been married before, but occasionally I will meet someone who is beginning a successful first marriage in their fifties. Vera met Roger when she was forty-eight. They dated for two years before they were married. When I met her, they had been happily married for two years and are going strong. So every story is as unique as the people in it. There's no right way to find the partnership you've been longing for—but it does happen all the time. We are all on different journeys that include struggles and successes that require different timing for falling in love.

Vera struggled with alcoholism and really made the decision when she was forty-eight that she wanted to get sober and stay sober. That year brought many needed changes into her life and was also the year she met Roger. She had been in recovery in the Los Angeles area for about five years and had a recent relapse that was triggered in part by a destructive relationship with a younger man who only wanted to use her. She went into rehab for a month and then sober living and then took a job that was dissatisfying. Her sponsor pointed out that her situation at work would not be healthy for her, so she started to look for alternatives. She moved out of Los Angeles to Palm Desert. It was a start. Her sister-in-law kidded cheerfully, "Don't worry. You're going to meet some great divorcee out there." She saw a job posting for a sales position—she had no training in this specific area, but something told her to take a closer look. Her background was in management and creative work in graphic design. The posting called for someone with a knowledge of sales and design—but this referred to interior design, so she didn't know what she was getting herself into. She went to the interview with her graphic design portfolio tucked under her arm figuring it couldn't hurt to showcase her talents. That day Roger interviewed her—he was the general manager of the company and, unbeknownst to either of them, her future husband. Looking back, he said he thought it was the cutest thing that she was enthusiastically carrying her artwork with her.

Roger asked her in for several more interviews and then he hired her. Everything was completely professional between them, but why had there been so many interviews? After the third interview, her dad said, "I think this guy really likes you." She replied, "Dad, I think he just really wants me to work for him." It wasn't long before Vera admitted that there was chemistry right from the start. As they worked together it grew. Still, Roger was her boss and a complete gentleman. He was old-fashioned and probably wouldn't have ever said anything about the connection that was building between them since she was his employee. Vera started to become renewed by the paths opening up in her life. She watched the movie *Silver Linings Playbook* and admired how the main characters struggled with so many things but were adamant about dancing and making their relationship work. In a moment of inspiration, she decided that she could take a chance to bring something positive into her life. There was no way she was just making up the sparks that she felt with Roger. So she decided to make the first move and tell him how she felt.

They were always texting about work, and she realized that she wanted to talk to him more. She didn't want to tell him what she was thinking over text message—it had to be in person. They were at work, and he was giving her some direct product knowledge training. She turned to him and said, "At lunch I need to talk to you," not knowing where her newfound courage came from. She knew that his marriage was over. She wouldn't have put herself out there otherwise. Ethically, this was so important to her that even now she struggles with the fact that he didn't have completed, signed divorce papers when they realized there was a connection between them. But Roger was a free man—he had been separated from his soon to be ex-wife for years, and he moved all the way across the country to fully end the relationship and build a whole new life and business. So at lunch, her courage still intact, she said to him, "I have to let you know that I feel like it's really important, almost like it's not about me. I feel that it's important that I let you know that I've never felt this way about anybody, that I'm very attracted to you." He didn't really get it at first. He said, "Attracted, attracted?" Vera replied, "Haven't you picked up on that? It's just so present." Did he really not realize or did he not want to admit it? Vera had learned to trust her intuition long ago, leading her to sometimes realize things before other people, once she even saved her dad from a house fire with perfectly spooky timing. So she knew now was another time to trust her gut. She continued, "I just needed to tell you, but I don't know what comes next." They just sat there and looked at each other for a long time. She had no idea what he was going to say. In the silence she imagined at any moment he would reply, "Thank you for telling me, but I'm not interested." She was so used to things not working out in her life that her expectations were low. She just wanted to get her feelings off her chest. He finally said "Well, what should we do about it?" in a suave tone.

It felt like the romance happened right away. She was still new to the job, and now they were planning to go out to dinner. The feelings between them were strong. He let her know that he never would have approached her since she was an employee. He wouldn't come right out and say that he felt the attraction too—he said that something like this had never happened to him before and that he was in shock and flattered and perhaps they should discuss it more over dinner. She apologized in case she had made him feel awkward. He said that was not the case and then finally said, "I have to admit I have been thinking about you." About a week later, they had their first date at a trendy restaurant in Palm Springs. They kissed goodnight, and it just clicked. He retired about three weeks later to eliminate the conflict with work interests. It was a very exciting time. When he quit, he told his coworkers that he had fallen for Vera and had to step away from the business.

Roger had previously been married for many years and had a strong sense of family and fidelity. Vera became his third wife. His first wife was the mother of his kids. They were married right out of high school but developed different lifestyles. She became a hippie artist type and asked for a divorce after they had been together twenty-three years. It was heartbreaking, and he turned to a close friend who soon became his second wife. They were together for eighteen years, and even though they had long been separated, it was hard for him to officially ask for a divorce until he met Vera and knew that's what he had to do. Perhaps it's not romantic to frame the sequence of events this way, but this is real life and the roads we travel to find each other are sometimes complicated.

Roger had moved across the country years earlier, to end his marriage and start over. However, he wasn't yet divorced. Vera is very generous to share with us. She's self-conscious over whether her relationship with Roger started in the "right" way. As she made her way through her relationship with Roger, she had to learn to trust herself and make healthy relationship choices. Her ability to question her own motives and check in with her moral compass proves she's on the right track.

As they continued to date, Vera started to struggle with her own need for independence. She lived her whole life ensuring that her own basic needs were met—dating someone who could potentially become a spouse was an entirely different situation. She always kept a roof over her head no matter what else was going on. She always made it work somehow. She was very set in her ways: She prized her private time and meditating. Moving in with Roger required her to learn to surrender. She started to worry that he was too controlling for her and considered walking out. Perhaps it was just that she had no practice cohabitating. So they went to couple's therapy while they were dating. So many good things were happening, and she did have a history of sabotaging relationships and opportunities. Something inside told her to stick with him. He abstains from drinking around her out of respect for her sobriety. They continued counseling and it was helpful—they were able to find a therapist for people who basically have a good life, but just want to get better. She knew she didn't want to ruin this partnership; she just wasn't used to being treated well. Roger also started attending Al-Anon: a program for the families of those who are alcoholics or in recovery. At first, he thought this would be a good way to figure Vera out, but what he learned actually helped him make sense of some of the hard things he had experienced growing up. His father had been a physician, and his mother had become a socially acceptable pill popper in the 1960s, which surely left some scars on his own life and the way he built relationships.

Keeping the balance in their relationship relied upon allowing Vera to have opportunities for independence and happily merging with Roger's strong family values and relationship with his children. At first, he said, "It's okay if you don't work. I will take you traveling." And they did travel a lot, but Vera needed a creative outlet and enjoyed working. He helped her start a freelance graphic design business, and then she found a job she truly loves selling designer clothes nearby. He couldn't stop being a hard worker either: he volunteered as a business mentor and ended up sometimes treating this like a regular job. Other times, they would travel. They went to Paris and Italy and visited his daughter in Ireland where she had married an Irish boy she met while studying abroad. They took a two-week trip up the coast of California. She connected with a lot of old friends, and it was very healing. When they came back down to Southern

California, she met Roger's kids. After this long trip, they continued to visit with Roger's kids nearly every weekend, and her relationship with them was really growing.

His boys and one step-daughter were always really nice to her. The other step-daughter was a bit more standoffish—she was the child of Roger's last wife and needed a little more time to warm up to Vera. She realizes that when anyone younger meets a man who clearly has a good amount of money, people might assume that's why she's interested. The gap between Vera and Roger is only ten years, but she thought his family might question her values. This was not the case. After meeting his kids, it was clear to them that she only wanted to bring more warmth to their family. It was a bit harder to be accepted by his friends. For Roger's sixtieth birthday, they planned a big party in Palm Desert. Vera's mom and dad were also in attendance. Roger's best friends came out from Wisconsin. They were very close with Roger's ex, and this created some tension. They stayed at his house for two weeks, and Vera couldn't break past one woman's rigid façade and animosity. They went out shopping. Then, they went to get their nails done together, which Roger wanted to pay for, so Vera brought along his credit card. As they were shopping, his friend would say things like, "Oh, you like that? Just buy it. It's not your money," which made Vera very uncomfortable and really felt like some kind of devious test. It didn't matter what this woman thought—Vera had honest intentions for a good relationship with Roger.

By the next Christmas, they were living together and trading off cooking. It felt like once Vera turned fifty, that something inside her finally allowed her to surrender. She thought to herself that she didn't want to be afraid anymore. She just wanted to trust herself. On December 23, she came home from work and the table was set and Roger was making a beautiful dinner of asparagus, steak, and Caesar salad from scratch. She thought it was strange that he wasn't in his usual casual attire but figured he just wanted their gift exchange to be special. He had already given her amazing gifts for other occasions by listening closely to things she mentioned she needed or liked. She was getting used to his romantic and thoughtful demeanor. After dinner they traded gifts, and she opened a lovely pashmina scarf, and then he handed her another box saying, "Well, I don't know if you're going to like this…" The box was long and thin, so she expected a necklace or a bracelet. She opened it and found a rhinestone tennis bracelet. She exclaimed, "Oh!" and he said, "I hope you like it." She was looking at it, thinking that it wasn't really her style, and she was almost positive it was made of rhinestones not diamonds. It was a little gaudy, so she was trying to feign interest. He said, "I can tell you're not happy with it. There's a charm that goes on it. I think it's underneath." She looked underneath, and the "charm" was all wrapped in tape. He said, "You'll have to pull it apart." It was so hard to get open she finally resorted to scissors. By now, she could tell something was going on and started to get excited. When she opened the bundle of packing and revealed an engagement ring, he said, "Will you marry me?" She was delighted and sighed "Oh my God, yes!" right away. She called her mom that night. He had asked her dad for her hand, so her parents already knew and they adored Roger. It was a neat, old-fashioned way to get engaged.

They set the date for September 19 of the coming year. Vera is the oldest daughter in her family, so her mother was very excited. Though she never spent much time imagining a fairytale wedding, this was her first marriage, and Vera was excited to do things her way. The wedding felt large to her—over one hundred people attended. It was especially important that her father walk her down the aisle. Her parents are in their eighties, but they have many healthy friends who have attended the family church for decades. It was significant to be able to get married in the church she grew up in surrounded by familiar faces. She asked her sister, sister-in-law, and one of her best friends from college to be her bridesmaids. She envisioned her perfect dress, and her dream came true. It was formal navy-blue Armani stunner, and no one batted an eye at her color choice because the dress was so amazing. The flowers were also just as she pictured.

They spent their honeymoon on a Mediterranean cruise. Aboard the ship, they were treated like king and queen. They went on day-long excursions, and she got to wear all her most beautiful clothes. They ended their four-week trip with four days in Barcelona feeling grounded and relaxed. When they returned home, they maintained their habit of taking long trips together. Her work lets her take time off since she is a highly valued employee. They recently went to the New Orleans Jazz Fest and trips to see Roger's kids are still a regular occurrence.

This family time has been one of the most rewarding aspects of their relationship. It was a big regret of hers that she never had kids, but she wanted to make sure that her life was in balance first and foremost. Once things started to stabilize in her life, she knew she had always really wanted to be a mom. Now Vera participates in the lives of Roger's many kids and grandkids. They love her, and she can share her life with them. She also got to keep her beautiful figure intact, whereas the rest of us have war wounds. Roger's grandkids are all under five, and she's pretty much been with them since they were born, so they know her as their grandma and call her GG. One of them called her on Mother's Day and said, "Happy GGs day." And this short conversation was probably the most fulfilling thing she's received in her life.

Vera didn't intentionally wait until she was over fifty to marry. It wasn't until she began to trust herself and learned to surrender to positive, loving situations that she became truly open to the possibility.

CONCLUSION

You Know It's Right When Everything Just Falls into Place

The women included in this book are all very different. It just goes to prove that anyone can find a successful second marriage. It doesn't matter if you're a stay-at-home mom or an executive—there's hope. The women in this book do share one important personality trait: confidence. Some were born with it, while others learned after their first marriages and the trials of life that they could prioritize their own needs and find someone who really completes them. Some learned to walk away from a broken relationship that was the cornerstone of their family life and, in doing so, proved to themselves that they are strong mothers and women. I believe that oftentimes we attract people with similar personality characteristics to our own—many of the strong, loving women in this book attracted strong, reliable, successful partners by taking the time between marriages, whether brief or long, to get very clear about what they wanted in a future mate. It also takes confidence in yourself to believe that a happy ending is possible, and I hope this book has shared that with you.

Another trend I've noticed in gathering the stories for this book is that if the guy has decided that being married is what he wants, it makes it much easier. Once he's sure, everything just falls into place. This is how it was for me and Michael. Michael is the perfect fit for me, but I don't know if I would have recognized that he was so great if he hadn't decided on me first. He could see it very clearly. We'd known each other for seventeen years, and he'd been my client all that time. When things shifted in his life after the end of his first marriage, he sought me out. We dated for a little over two years before he proposed. Surprisingly, Michael also took the lead on planning our destination wedding.

He said the decision of what type of wedding to have was up to me—we discussed going to somewhere exotic, just the two of us to exchange vows. I wanted to have my kids there and his daughter. So we decided on a small family gathering in Hawaii, still exotic but much more manageable in terms of travel and having our nearest and dearest with us. Just for the fun of it and because he travels so much, Michael has a travel agent's license, so he did the actual organizing of the wedding. He would check in with me on the details. However, in no way did this resemble the kind of planning many of us do for our first weddings. The first time around I was impossible—wanting very specific details. This time, it was more about the excitement of finding a true partner, and he was already giving me exactly what I wanted: to have my kids there. He felt that it was important that celebration was memorable, not the usual big fairy tale white wedding of my youth, but with lots of beautiful touches. We decided we like Maui best, and he contacted a wedding planner in Hawaii. I picked out the photographer, and together we selected a minister and all the music, including specific songs that we both liked. I picked the flowers and the cake, so we were always checking in with each other, but in general he organized and ran the event.

In learning the stories of women who remarry, I have noticed that the emphasis is not so much on the wedding itself. Instead, we share the excitement of building a new partnership, which is something that extends well beyond the wedding day and is so much more valuable. Perhaps this is why so many of the women I talked to decided to have unique and intimate celebrations. Aurora enjoyed a Vegas wedding that her younger self never would have realized could be so much fun. Several of the women enjoyed cruises, receptions, and dinners that allowed them to extend the day of celebration and spend time with all the different groups of people in their lives. Even Vera, who was married for the first time in her fifties, opted for a stunning dark blue gown over the traditional white ensemble. Just like each partnership, each wedding reflected a new outlook and enjoyment of life. I see so much hope in these stories.

After sharing major transitions from their first marriages, some of the hardships of being single, and the in-between times of waiting and wondering in this book, I am so happy to also share our celebrations with you. We deserve to hear those stories too, the ones that prove that it's very likely that if you want to get remarried, it will happen for you. You should just enjoy your life until your time comes. Take care of yourself and do the things you need for your own growth. When you are ready, it will also happen for you.

ABOUT THE AUTHOR

Autumn Marie is an accomplished business-woman with an established track record of success. She currently works for a leading title & escrow company in the California real estate industry.

She is a leader in her community and church, as well as a devoted mother of two, along with a daughter-in-law and a new step-daughter and son-in-law. Autumn's children have always been her highest priority in life. Her son is a U.S. Navy war veteran and her daughter a project manager for a major Fortune 500 organization. Autumn and Michael are immensely proud of all of their children and were thrilled to welcome their first grandchild into the world in January 2018. Autumn is very excited to be a new "Glamma" as she affectionately likes to be called. Autumn lives in San Diego, California, alongside her loving husband, Michael. Together they are a true success story in both business and romance.

CPSIA information can be obtained
at www.ICGtesting.com
Printed in the USA
LVHW112054290419
616026LV00005B/556/P